OPTIMIZING DISCOVERY SYSTEMS TO IMPROVE USER EXPERIENCE

**Recent Titles in Libraries Unlimited's
Innovative Librarian's Guide Series**

Digitizing Audiovisual and Nonprint Materials:
The Innovative Librarian's Guide
Scott Piepenburg

Making the Most of Digital Collections through Training
and Outreach: The Innovative Librarian's Guide
Nicholas Tanzi

Digitizing Your Community's History:
The Innovative Librarian's Guide
Alex Hoffman

Customizing Vendor Systems for Better User Experiences:
The Innovative Librarian's Guide
Matthew Reidsma

OPTIMIZING DISCOVERY SYSTEMS TO IMPROVE USER EXPERIENCE

The Innovative Librarian's Guide

Bonnie Imler and Michelle Eichelberger

INNOVATIVE LIBRARIAN'S GUIDE

LIBRARIES UNLIMITED™

An Imprint of ABC-CLIO, LLC

Santa Barbara, California • Denver, Colorado

Library of Congress Cataloging in Publication Control Number: 2017004286

ISBN: 978-1-4408-4382-2
EISBN: 978-1-4408-4383-9

21 20 19 18 17   1 2 3 4 5

This book is also available as an eBook.

Libraries Unlimited
An Imprint of ABC-CLIO, LLC

ABC-CLIO, LLC
130 Cremona Drive, P.O. Box 1911
Santa Barbara, California 93116-1911
www.abc-clio.com

This book is printed on acid-free paper ∞

Manufactured in the United States of America

Contents

Acknowledgments		ix
Introduction		xi
Chapter 1	Setting the Stage	1
Chapter 2	Usability Testing	5
	Usability Testing Framework	6
	Creating the Study Team	8
	Defining the Purpose of the Study	9
	Defining the Scope of the Study	10
	Identifying Participants	10
	Selecting a Study Method	15
	Designing Your Instrument	16
	Selecting a Data Collection Method	26
	Creating Consent Forms	35
	Seeking Permission for the Study	35
	Recruiting Participants	36
	Planning Research Session Details	39
	Conducting Testing	40
	Collecting Data	40
	Data Analysis	41
	Report Findings	43
	Instrument and Data Retention	44
	Storage Methods for Study Instruments and Results	45
	Study Follow Through	46
Chapter 3	Discovery System Configuration	47
	Data Decisions	48
	The Catalog	49
	Local Catalog Data	49
	External Catalog Data	51
	Local Catalog Tools	51
	Databases	52

		Recommended Database Option in Summon	52
		Database Selection and Branding	53
	eBook Collections		54
	Setting Up Your User Interface		55
		Search Decisions	55
		Results List	56
		Getting to Full Text	62
	Website Access to the Discovery System		64
		Benchmarking against Other Libraries	65
		Search Box Design	65
	Web Implementation		67
		Beta Testing	67
		System Deployment	69
		Transition Planning	69
	Search Engine Optimization		71
Chapter 4	Library Instruction and Discovery Systems		73
	Instruction Methods		74
		Learning Outcomes	74
		Where to Start	75
		Keyword vs. Subject Searching	76
		Advanced Search	77
		Boolean Quotation Marks and Truncation	78
		Teaching to Limit	80
		Teaching the Extras	87
		Citation	90
		Discovery System Help	90
		Promoting the Library Reference Desk	91
		Teaching Library Research Grit	92
Chapter 5	PR and Community Buy-In		97
	Naming Your Discovery System		97
		What's in a Name?	98
		Naming Decisions	99
		Name Longevity	101
	Discovery System PR		102
		PR Leadership	102
		PR Methods	103
	Discovery System Orientation		115
		Promotional Timing	115
	Community Buy-In		116
		Library Staff	116
		Selling To Faculty	117
		Student Buy-In	121

Chapter 6   Conclusion   123
               You Have the Power   123
               A Moving Target   124

Appendix: Software and Tools   125
Glossary   127
Bibliography   129
Index   131

Acknowledgments

First, thank you to Libraries Unlimited, ABC-CLIO, for giving us the opportunity to write this book. Thanks to Lise Dyckman for recruiting us for the project and to Emma Bailey for guiding us through the process.

Michelle would like to thank the State University of New York Librarians Association and the State University of New York Office of Library and Information Services, both of which have provided her with opportunities to learn more about discovery systems through listservs, conferences, and web discussion. Bonnie would like to thank Binky Lush for sharing her incredible discovery system expertise.

Bonnie is appreciative to Penn State University and the University Libraries administration for allowing her a sabbatical to complete this project. She would like to thank the staff of the Penn State Altoona Robert E. Eiche Library for all of their encouragement for the book project and for all their hard work while she was on sabbatical. Special thanks to Mary Lou Patrick for taking over as Acting Library Director in her absence. Bonnie would also like to thank her friends and family who kept asking about the progress of the book and especially her husband Jeff and sons Gabe and Kendrick for their love, patience, and support.

Michelle would like to thank her colleagues at the SUNY Genesee Community College Alfred C. O'Connell Library for their encouragement and support during the writing process. Library Director Nina Warren has been especially gracious in allowing Michelle the time and flexibility to write while also performing her day-to-day duties. Michelle is also thankful for the interest and enthusiasm about the book from her friends and family, with special thanks for Lance Topping's love and support. Last, but definitely not least, Michelle would like to thank coauthor Bonnie Imler for giving her the opportunity to work on this book, and she is also grateful for her many years of friendship and scholarly collaboration. Bonnie is one of the few people who could ask Michelle "Want to write a book?" and get an immediate positive response, no questions asked.

Introduction

Discovery Systems have been widely adopted as library research tools, but what if you've set one up at your library and it's not working how you'd like it to work, or it's not as popular with your patrons as you think it could or should be? How can you make it easier to use and get your money's worth out of it? This book is here to help. It will provide you with:

- Usability testing methods that you can use to identify the strengths and weaknesses of your Discovery System
- Advice for configuring your under-the-hood system settings to maximize ease of use and effectiveness for your patrons
- Learning outcomes and lesson ideas that you can use to improve library instruction about your Discovery System
- Tips on ways to encourage administration, staff, and community buy-in in order to get more use out of your system
- Best practices for publicizing and marketing your system

This book will show you how to implement User Experience (UX) studies to examine how your discovery systems are being used, which will give you data and observations that you can share with your colleagues and funding bodies, in order to inform decisions about enhancing, promoting, and teaching discovery systems.

Why should we care about discovery systems and making them better? One word: Google. It's getting harder to sell library databases to patrons as the best place to start when doing research because students, faculty, and community members are familiar with and comfortable using Internet search engines and websites. Google, as a for-profit company, has invested time and money into creating search algorithms that are much more effective and intuitive than library catalog or database searching. Google can spell-check your search and fix it for you. Google can suggest a topic that you might be searching for based on the first few characters that you type. Google can match search results to your location. Bottom line: using Google is easy.

All libraries face the challenge of encouraging patrons to use the resources that have been paid for by the library. In the academic library, trying to persuade students to use library resources instead of Google can be an uphill climb, especially with first-year students. These students may not need the serious, scholarly resources required for assignments in upper level classes and may feel that Google results are good enough. With the growing amount of scholarly information freely available online, it's possible that sometimes the students are correct and what they find in Google will meet their research needs. These same students may not receive library instruction, and if they do attend an instruction session, they may not believe that it's relevant to their assignments. Community members may have the same reluctance to use a somewhat complicated library database interface instead of Google, even if they're trying to find reputable, scholarly information about a health concern or other topic. How do we lure these patrons into the library databases? Single search box discovery systems, that's how.

Chapter 1

Setting the Stage

Single–search box technology began to emerge in the library field in the mid-2000s, with federated search systems like Ex Libris's MetaLib and Serials Solutions' 360 Search. These early forays into search consolidation were not particularly successful. Performing searches in these systems was a slow process, because the software was designed to live-search multiple websites, rather than searching a canned data repository. The relevancy ranking for results was poor, and the website design wasn't intuitive. For those of you who were required to promote these tools, you'll remember that it was often a hard sell to get patrons to use them, even if we knew the benefits of searching more than one database at a time. Students, faculty, and librarians found the federated search systems clunky to use, but they were a step in the right single-search direction. In the late 2000s, more modern systems began to appear on the scene, including OCLC's Worldcat Local (released in November 2007), Serials Solutions' Summon (July 2009), EBSCO's EBSCO Discovery System (EDS; January 2010), and Ex Libris's Primo Central (June 2010).

At the time of this writing, the best-selling discovery systems are EBSCO's EDS, Proquest's The Summon Service, Ex Libris Primo, and OCLC's Worldcat Discovery Services. In academic libraries, EBSCO's EDS has the greatest number of installations, then Primo, Summon, and WorldCat Discovery, while public libraries tend to implement the service created by the provider of their integrated library system (ILS; Breeding, 2016). Marshall Breeding, a top researcher and writer in the field of library technology, lists other major discovery products on his Library Technology Guides website: AquaBrowser, Biblio Commons, VuFind, SirsiDynix, and more (Breeding, "Library Technology Guides"). Major vendors like EBSCO have set up partnerships where libraries can choose to use either their own current catalog user interface or EBSCO's EDS as their front end. The list of vendors with whom EBSCO partners include SirsiDynix, OCLC, UNIBIS, Archimedes, and others (EBSCO, "ILS Partners").

It's important to note that this book is not meant to be an exhaustive review of all the discovery systems available on the market. The topics of usability, configuration, instruction, and promotion can be applied to any discovery system, but the authors are most familiar with EBSCO's EDS and Proquest's Summon products, and it is from these two systems that most of our examples will be drawn. Marshall Breeding and other experts in the field have done a great job in keeping up with trends in discovery system implementation and usage, and their publications are available online and in library publications including *Library Journal, Computers in Libraries*, and *College & Research Libraries*.

The goal of all of the discovery systems is to make most, if not all, of a library's proprietary content searchable from a single search box. This content can include catalog records, database content, digital collections, and local repository collections. One of the best features of discovery systems is that they can provide access to indexing for content even if that content is not part of the vendor's holdings, meaning that library patrons can get search results for a huge variety of content even if the library does not pay for that content. With careful implementation of link resolvers and interlibrary loan, patrons can now get access to more research material than ever possible in the past.

As noted by JoLinda Thompson in her book *Implementing Web-Scale Discovery Services: A Practical Guide for Librarians* (Thompson, 2014), common features of discovery systems include:

- Relevancy ranking of results
- Faceting or clustering limiters
- "Did you mean?" search suggestions or spell-checking
- Direct links to full-text content, either from the vendor or via a link resolver system like EBSCO's Full-text Finder, or SFX
- Record management features such as citation tools, permalinks, user accounts for result management
- Links to social media sites
- Optional Web 2.0 features including user reviews and tags

Discovery system vendors are constantly working on adding new features to their products, and adding new ways that their content and search results can be integrated into other library products like Springshare's LibGuides, or other educational software like the course management systems Blackboard and Moodle. Here are few of the new features:

- **Chat integration**: Chat can be embedded as a pop-up, a static widget, or a simple image link.
- **Cloud data management**: Patrons can save articles or results lists directly to their Google Drive accounts or other cloud storage locations.
- **Better WMS integration**: Patrons can place holds on their library's materials via the discovery system.
- **Course management integration**: Faculty can create reading lists for their students in Blackboard using EBSCO's Curriculum Builder tool, and Summon offers a similar service through the SIPX Reading List Module at an additional add-on cost.

- **LibGuides integration**: EBSCO lets you pull EDS search results into your guides and Summon allows you to highlight related research guides on the results page.
- **Autocorrect**: Discovery system vendors are working on Google-like autocorrect, "did you mean?" results.
- **Enhanced social media**: Google books and Goodreads integration.

It can be a challenge for librarians to keep up with all the changes and improvements in the discovery system world, but it's an even bigger challenge to make sure that your current system is working the way you want it to work. The next chapter will give you the tools that you need to design and implement effective and efficient usability testing.

Chapter 2

Usability Testing

Usability testing is the best way to take the pulse of your discovery system and see how it's being used by your patrons. Usability testing in the library seems like something that would be an obvious task, since most libraries wouldn't exist without their patrons, and we want to keep our patrons happy and keep them coming back to the library. However, just because we are all about user experience, trying to put ourselves in our users' shoes can be difficult for many reasons. We may think that we know what our users need and how they experience our libraries, but without real, unbiased usability testing, we may be fooling ourselves. Planning comprehensive and effective usability studies can take staff time, funding, and hard work, and it can be overwhelming. This chapter will give you some concrete places to start, or to help refine, your UX journey.

It's important to note that discovery systems are not created in a vacuum by vendors who are completely out of touch with what their customers need and want. EBSCO employs a User Research group to test their products on real customers, stating that "creating products that are based on an understanding of customer and user needs is at the heart of EBSCO's mission" (EBSCO Information Services).

Summon is also highly interested in the usability of their product and provides an online wiki for the Summon community with links to reports on usability studies performed at Summon sites as well as shared scripts designed to help you conduct your own usability testing. However, just because the vendors are trying to create products that meet the needs of the majority of their customers, this doesn't mean that you shouldn't do your own usability testing. You'll have a lot of control over how you set up your system locally, and you need to make sure that your decisions are the best ones for your patrons.

A word that comes up frequently when defining user experience is "actual." How do users *actually* navigate our library systems? Can they *actually* complete online tasks to the desired outcome? What do users *actually* want? What do they *actually* expect the library to offer? Are they *actually* satisfied with our brick and click environments? Patrons' *actual* requirements are usually drastically different from what we perceive and expect them to be. The cool new interface design implemented by the web guru at the discovery system company may not be as useful to your patrons as the vendor hopes it will be. Our web pages filled with library jargon and research paths designed by well-meaning librarians with the goal of turning every patron into a world class researcher may not help our patrons as well as we expected. In this day of high competition from the open web, each design choice matters, and all of our good intentions mean little if our users are frustrated and irritated when they attempt to navigate our discovery systems.

User experience is critical for libraries and librarians because it provides both the tools for real-life, actual assessment and results in explicit data that can be used to drive change in your library. Without formal usability testing, librarians can observe user interaction with our systems, but without concrete data, it's difficult to react to your observations and make substantial changes to your discovery system interface or web navigation. Positive results from a usability test reinforce that you are on the right track, and negative results give you a clear direction for improvement.

Usability testing is the best way to monitor the effectiveness of your discovery system. It can be used to determine user response to the system's overall look and feel, the system's searchability, and the ability of the user to achieve their end goal, which is to find credible information about a particular topic or question. Every librarian should care about the experience of their users, and we should put at least as much time studying our online environment as we do making improvements to physical collections, facilities, and signage in our library buildings.

So, where do you start? Usability testing tools can cost thousands of dollars in a one-time fee, a monthly or yearly subscription rate, the cost of a pack of paper and printing, or it can be absolutely free. The complexity of the testing can range from sophisticated eye-tracking and screen capture coding software, to a one-question survey kept at the library service desk for patrons to complete while they're waiting to check materials in or out. Whatever type of testing you decide to do, from simple forms to high-tech testing, the following Usability Testing Framework can help you focus and clarify your study.

USABILITY TESTING FRAMEWORK

- Create the study team.
- Define the purpose of the study.
- Define the scope of the study.
- Determine type and number of participants.
- Investigate and select a study method.
- Design your instrument.
- Select a data collection method.

- Compose consent form.
- Seek permission from institutional review board (IRB) or governing bodies if necessary (they will want to see your study materials, consent form, etc.).
- Recruit participants.
- Plan research session details.
- Conduct testing.
- Collect data.
- Analyze data.
- Report findings.
- Make data retention decisions.
- Follow through with improvements to the site.

This list may seem daunting, but it can be easily tailored to fit your needs. Are you planning to present each patron with a choice of two names for your discovery system while they're waiting at a service desk? If so, you will not need to ask them to sign a consent form or formally recruit participants. Are you only interested in reviewing your site analytics? Then, you won't need to select or recruit participants. This usability testing framework is comprehensive, but each bullet point is not mandatory.

Before you begin a usability study, you'll need to explore whether or not your institution requires you to follow guidelines that regulate the study or surveying of human participants. At the college/university level, this may mean that you'll need to seek approval from an IRB, which can take time, and may require extra effort to fill out forms and/or pursue research training. If this is the case, you'll need to plan your study timing accordingly. At the elementary/high school level, your study may require administrative or school board approval, and at the public library it may mean checking into whether your usability testing will violate any of your own policies that prohibit solicitation in the library.

When working on getting approval for your usability study, the key factors are the two Cs: confidentiality and consent. The ideal usability test is one in which study participants participate willingly, with little or no risk that sensitive or personal information will be publicly released by the researchers. For a study to be truly confidential, a number of questions need to be considered thoroughly before starting the study:

Administration: Who will administer the usability study? How many people will collect the data?

Analysis: Who will be allowed to see the collected data? Who will do the data analysis?

Results: Who will see the study results? Will they be allowed to share the results with others?

Storage: Where will the study data be stored? Will the location be locked? Will the identifying information be removed?

Retention: For how long will the data be stored?

If you work for an academic institution that requires IRB approval, you will be asked to answer all of the previous questions, and probably many more, before the study is approved. You may also be required to attend an online or in-person training course that reviews federal and ethical considerations of working with human subjects. In some cases, you will be required to pass a test, indicating your understanding of these principles and policies.

Creating the Study Team

Once you've gained the necessary approval for your study, it's time to put together your study team. The makeup of your team is crucial to the success of your study because too few team members can lead you to miss out on important details that you want to cover in the study, but too many members can cause you to get bogged down in lengthy discussions about wording and other design options. In order to streamline your usability study, study design works best as the responsibility of one person, or at the most, a small team. However, your study will be most effective if you can gather initial discovery system feedback and ideas from a wide range of your library staff, most importantly from those on the frontline who assist your users every day.

Input from your peers can help you focus your usability study on problem areas of the discovery system that have been reported anecdotally, but for which you do not have any concrete data to show your administration and/or those who have the power to make changes to the system. Here are some questions that you can use to help you gather general discovery system feedback from library staff, reference librarians, and instruction librarians:

- Do you find that many patrons don't know where to start searching on our library website?
- If they do know where to start, are they using the discovery system, or are they going to a specific database or the catalog?
- Is there one particular place where you've seen users get stuck in the discovery process?
- If so, how do you instruct them to proceed?
- Are patrons able to print/retrieve the content that they need? Or do you find piles of printouts around your printers, implying that your patrons left them there when they found that it wasn't the full-text content that they thought they had printed?

Reviewing your library staff's perceived use of the discovery system can help you begin to narrow down the areas that you'd like to cover in your study. Involving all of your staff in the discovery planning process can help you get buy-in from these people during the study, and can help you to make sure that you don't miss any important aspects of your patrons' discovery system experience.

Defining the Purpose of the Study

All of the usability testing methods described in this chapter require the researcher to have a clearly delineated sense of what they intend to study. Defining the study takes some time and thought, and it is different from creating a hypothesis or predicting outcomes. The study definition should consist of a positive purpose statement rather than one that is more negative because if you take a negative direction, it can lead to a study design that skews your results negatively.

Positive study purpose examples:
- This study will determine if users can easily find the full text of an article.
- This study will determine if users can locate local, historical, newspaper articles.
- This study will determine if users are more likely to click on limit links, if they are on a bright blue or a muted gray background.

As you can see, the purpose statement can range from a vague and open statement, or it can be quite specific.

Negative study purpose examples:
- This study will prove that users do not view nonunderlined text as links.
- This study will prove that known citation searches are difficult for patrons.
- This study will show that the discovery system link resolver software is hard to use.

These negative purpose statements may be based on real-life problems that have been observed and reported by librarians, but they do not have to define the study itself. If these negative statements accurately describe problems with your system, these trouble areas will still be evident even if you design a study with a positive purpose, such as these examples:

Revised negative study purpose examples:
- This study will review how well users are able to identify and use discovery system links.
- This study will examine how patrons find results for a specific citation.
- This study will determine how patrons use the discovery system link resolver software.

The benefit of using a positive study purpose will be that you will have not biased the outcomes by focusing on the negative results in your data analysis. The goal is to design an exploratory study that captures the real way that your patrons use your system, instead of setting your participants up for failure.

Defining the Scope of the Study

The scale of your testing will determine the methods that you choose to incorporate. You may only want to perform small-scale testing on one tiny, but crucial, part of your discovery system design. Examples of this small scope testing areas are:

- Choosing the best, easiest to navigate, background color for your system
- Identifying patron preference for underlined vs. nonunderlined links
- Analyzing which limiter terms are most clearly understood and identifiable for your patrons (e.g., "scholarly articles" vs. "peer-reviewed articles")

At the other end of the testing spectrum, you may want to take a look at the big picture of how your system is being used, but keep in mind that the broader you make the scope of your testing, the more data you'll have to analyze. It's easy to get bogged down in results, and too much data can mean that the results never get analyzed and changes never get made to improve your system, which is the whole point of doing the testing. Examples of big picture testing questions are:

- How effectively are your patrons using the discovery system to find appropriate research sources for their assignments?
- How well do your students interact with the Discovery System web pages? Are they able to find the search box and other pertinent links?
- How does your web design affect user success rate in meeting their research needs?

Big picture testing examines how well users are able to use your system to complete their research goals. This type of testing should answer questions about overall user satisfaction and ease of use of the discovery system.

Identifying Participants

Depending on your library type and location, your user population may vary widely by age, race, educational background, gender, and many other demographics. Or, your library may serve a very specific population, such as doctors and staff in a hospital library or lawyers in a law library. You will need to decide on the type and number of participants that you wish to study. Here are some things to consider:

- If you work in a college library and you would like to study student use of your system, which students should you study? Undergraduates? First-year students? Graduate students? Should you include faculty?
- If you work in a multicampus college setting, should you study one campus, all campuses, a sampling of campuses?
- Should the study participants be long-time library users or first-timers?

- If you work in a public library, do you want to study patrons who are very comfortable using computers? Those with limited computer knowledge? Local students who use your library? Native English speakers and non-native speakers? And so on.
- Do you only want to study patrons who have already used your discovery system or those who have never seen it?
- Do you want to talk to patrons who prefer to use Google rather than the library's discovery tools or avid library users?

There are valid reasons for including or excluding any of these populations, but this is a crucial decision to make in the very preliminary stages of study design.

Personas

When considering who you want to include in your usability study, it can be helpful to create personas, or what Ardath Albee calls "a composite sketch, representative of a segment of your target market" (Muldoon, 2012). It is perhaps easiest to think of a persona as an avatar, a personification of a type of library user. Personas can be created by one person, or a small group, as long as the group is composed of those who work most closely with the full spectrum of library users, so that you can be sure that you're getting a full picture of the typical user for each category. The purpose of creating a set of personas is to further investigate our users' needs and wants, and to give us a means to reflect on how each type of user might react to the interfaces and navigation we put into place for our discovery systems.

To start creating personas, you should first identify your user base or audiences. You may have done this in a vague sort of way for other initiatives, but now you will want to be very specific. For example, in a public library, if you normally divide your users by age (children, teen, young adult, adult, senior citizens), you will want to examine each general audience for differences in how they use the library building, its services, and its collections. Some populations you may want to focus on are:

- Patrons who attend programming or use the community room for meetings but don't utilize the collection
- Homeschooled students
- Job seekers and others

While you can't create a persona for each individual user in your library, you do want to be sure that you have a good representation of your user base. Here are some things to consider:

- Gender
- Age

- Educational level
- Technology comfort level
- Physical or learning disabilities
- College student demographics:
  - What is their major?
  - Are they honors students or on academic probation, or must take additional core classes to meet base requirements?
  - Undergraduate or graduate?
  - Traditional, nontraditional, international?
  - Commuter, on-campus, or online?
- Faculty demographics:
  - Subject area?
  - New, mid-career, near retirement?
  - Tenured, tenure track, fixed term, or adjunct?

Once you have selected the number and type of personas to create, it is helpful to create a basic template to aid in the creation of your library personas. Here are some categories you may want to include on the template:

- A picture (stock photo or cartoon image)
- Fictional name (first only)—Eventually it will become easier to refer to "John" rather than "the mid-career faculty member in the College of Engineering."
- Age
- Gender
- General category (child, teen, student, faculty)
- Back story (three or four paragraphs that summarize details about the persona's life)
- Previous library experience (include personas with considerable experience and others that have seldom darkened the door of a library)
- Technology comfort level (include all levels from Luddite to cutting edge, early adaptor)
- Library needs (what is this type of person expecting from the library?)

SAMPLE PERSONA

Sara, Faculty New Hire
Sara is a new tenure track faculty member in the English Department.

Backstory

Sara is in her first year at the university. She is not an alumnus of this institution. She teaches mostly lower-level undergraduate courses. She regularly assigns projects to create blogs or other digital objects. She also requires a final research paper that is a more traditional five to seven-page paper. Sara is going through the tenure process and must publish and meet all additional requirements of tenure.

Use Case

Requires students to write a research paper using 10 scholarly resources, but assumes students know how to locate and use scholarly information. After her first semester, she was disappointed with the poor quality of references used in completed assignments.

Library Experience

- Uses only select eJournals from the library
- Does the majority of searching for other research information in Google Scholar
- Still trying to navigate the library web page and is expecting resources to have the same names as those she used at the university from which she graduated

When creating personas, it can be tempting to base them on an individual. Be sure that your personas are composites, and that another person familiar with your library couldn't look at the persona and say, "Oh, that's Professor Dean!" Also, be careful of stereotyping, such as creating an Asian persona whose main characteristic is that he or she is good at math and science or creating an older persona who is afraid of technology. Try to create real, unique personas that may reflect trends but are not bound by them.

If you're having trouble fine-tuning your personas, you can use data gathered from live participants in focus groups or other types of studies. Using information extracted from focus groups can enhance the accuracy of your personas and prevent them from becoming exaggerated stereotypes. It may help to hold a mixed-audience focus group before creating your personas to get yourself in tune with the needs of each user group and to add any insights gleaned from the focus group session to your personas. For example, an older individual in a focus group may mention that they don't like when the computer screen gets all "cluttered" and they can't find where they were before. It would be a good thing to note in your personal information that this type of user tends to be confused by links opening into new windows.

While you want to make sure that your user base is adequately represented, refrain from creating too many personas. The main goal is to be able to review these personas after you make a change to the discovery system and try to guess how each user group would react to the change. You are never going to make all of your users happy, but reviewing the personas may jog your memory about a particular user need that could be easily tweaked before your updates are rolled out.

Sample Size

Whether you plan to study personas or real people, you must determine how many participants you would like to include in your study. While it was once thought that a large number of study participants was needed to show all possible variations in thinking and preference, more recent research has concluded that the same results can be obtained with a much smaller sampling (Nielson, 2006). It is difficult to determine a specific acceptable sample size because that depends on the total number of individuals in your target population. Large populations need larger samples, but even a small population requires enough participants to adequately capture the group's thoughts and needs.

Having a true sample of the population is important to get a comprehensive understanding of your population(s), and it's also necessary to use correct sampling methods if you hope to publish your results in a scholarly journal.

Sample Method

If your study results are going to be published or otherwise highly scrutinized, you will want to conduct a formal sampling. In a formal sampling, you need to first identify your target population. The target population can be broadly defined, such as "all library users with a registered library card," or it could be a small group such as "all parents of preschoolers who attend library story time." The idea behind sampling is that every member of the population would be an adequate participant, so you only need a percentage of the population to get an acceptable picture of the beliefs and needs of the entire group. Random sampling is considered to be the most unbiased method of determining sample participants from the larger group. Here's an example of how to create a random sample: place all participant names on individual slips of paper in a basket and pick out names until the sample size has been met. If you're picking from a large population, you can work with your campus IT department or other IT staff to run programs to pick random participants, or you can use random number generators on the Internet to help you select your participants.

Here are a few things to consider when coordinating a random sample for a study:

Privacy: Obtaining the names and contact information for your target population may be the most difficult part of your entire study. You will want to carefully scrutinize the fine print on your library cards and registration documentation for wording concerning the use or distribution of private patron information. Additional permission to use personal data may also need to be obtained from a higher administrative body. Be especially vigilant about obtaining parental/guardian permission to survey minors.

Extra participants: You can decide on the perfect sample size for your study only to find that more than half of those contacted refuse to participate. For this reason, you will want to either increase your sample size from the start or keep a list of alternates if the initial sample size isn't met.

The most common form of sampling for library usability studies is much less stringent than a formal random sampling. It is a convenience sampling, which can be defined as selecting participants by their location at a given time, such as library users in your library at the time you have designated to work on your study. Convenience sampling can also be implemented online, by selecting patrons who happen to be using your website at the time you set your online poll to appear.

Regardless of your sample size or methods of obtaining it, when broadly surveying multiple populations, you will want to try to reach equal percentages of each population so that you can compare results fairly across categories. For example, if staff at a public library recruit 12 participants over the age of 50, 10 participants aged 20–50, one participant aged 13–19, and 11 under the age of 12, their teenage population will not be adequately represented in the study findings. Sometimes additional questions may need to be asked early in the recruiting process to prevent one subgroup from dominating your results. For example, when polling high school students, you may want to inquire whether students are homeschooled, cyberschooled, or if they attend a private or public school, so that you can be sure to gather a statistically valid sample from each group.

Selecting a Study Method

You will need to decide very early in your usability testing planning if your study will be quantitative, qualitative, or a little of both. When considering your options, it can help to review what you hope to gain from carrying out your usability study. In some cases, it will be important to have numbers and percentages to persuade an administrative body to invest in discovery system add-ons or to convince an implementation team that time and effort needs to put into improving the system. In other cases, you may simply want to use your results to help persuade your colleagues to do a better job of promoting the discovery system, and anecdotal evidence may be enough to help you plead your case.

If you will need to present statistical analysis to your stakeholders, you will want to conduct a quantitative study. Quantitative research looks for ways to measure people's behaviors and opinions in a way that can be turned into reliable statistics. These studies must be very structured, and it is extremely important that multiple researchers follow the same guidelines so that results are not skewed. Online and print polls and surveys are common quantitative methods, particularly those with questions asking the participant to choose or rank their selections. For example, if you design a poll that asks users to choose from four discovery system name options, you will be able to present quantitative name choice results to your administration and peers, such as which name ranked the highest and which ranked the lowest. Another quantitative study example would be a survey that asks participants to use a Likert scale to rank the discovery system's font color from 1 to 5 where 1 is strongly dislike and 5 is strongly like. Presenting a numeric result of something like an average of 4.7 for 30 participants in favor of a particular color might have more decision-making weight for your system designers than anecdotal evidence that your patrons prefer a different font color.

Qualitative studies tend to be much less structured and more exploratory in nature than quantitative studies. They have a less rigid scientific bent and more of a feeling, sensing approach. Common types of qualitative research are focus groups and observation of participant behavior. Researchers who use these methods often look for trends and encourage their participants to share their thought patterns and opinions. Qualitative studies are more likely to include human contact with the researcher, because they are intended to extract as much information as possible, which often requires follow-up questions. While the results in quantitative studies are usually numbers and percentages that can be easily displayed in charts, qualitative results can be presented with long bulleted lists of personal comments by individuals or descriptive case studies of individual users. Qualitative results can be summarized but usually not quantified, unless all participants exhibited the same behavior.

Some studies can be designed as hybrid studies, with a combination of quantitative and qualitative attributes. For example, an observational study can include the following research tasks:

- Track start and finish times for each task
- Record search behavior trends
- Ask the participants to describe their experience

This hybrid type of study will result in both numerical and qualitative data, and provide results that can be tailored to meet the statistical and narrative data needs of various library constituents.

Designing Your Instrument

As you read through this chapter, you might be thinking, "My library is small, understaffed, underfunded, and we don't have time to worry about qualitative vs. quantitative methods. We just want our discovery system to work better for our patrons, and we don't have the resources for a full-blown usability study." If a full-blown usability study is not possible in your library due to a shortage of staff, a lack of individuals with significant expertise in usability, or a shortage of staff time, here are two guerilla methods of usability testing: heuristic evaluation and cognitive walkthrough.

Heuristic evaluation is commonly done by a single member of your staff, preferably a person who has some experience with usability principles, and it's a way to determine if your discovery system user interface complies with certain usability principles, many of which are outlined in Jakob Nielsen's book *Usability Engineering* (1994). If you do not have an individual with this knowledge on your staff, you may want to contact a local college or university library to see if a usability-trained librarian would be willing to do your review. Frankly, some of these best practices, or heuristics, will seem very common sense in nature, but we spell them out here because they are often overlooked. They include:

- Minimalistic design, which helps keep your site easy to use for patrons
- Clear and consistent use of language
- The ability to quickly navigate back to a previous screen when a selection is made by mistake
- Sufficient help-type documentation that is easy to access

Heuristic evaluation reviews the "big picture" of the site and checks for glaring problems that might cause users to stumble in their research process. It can be good to perform a heuristic evaluation even if you are planning to do further usability testing, in order to catch and correct problems with the overall site before the testing takes place.

The cognitive walkthrough inspection method does not ignore the kinds of site errors found in heuristic evaluation, but its focus is on the usability of the paths for the common tasks performed on the site, such as looking for the full text of an article. A cognitive walkthrough outlines the various steps needed for a user to complete a certain task. For example, here are the steps that a patron would take to find a full-text article:

- Find the discovery system search box
- Enter the search
- Identify an article on your topic
- Find the full text of that article
- Print or save that full text

Cognitive walkthrough will demonstrate how the system should respond in an ideal research situation and how it would react if a patron makes an error or if a step is missed. In a cognitive walkthrough, it is important to track whether or not there are enough visual cues for the user to know how to proceed, and how to backtrack if they go down the wrong path. It's useful to conduct a cognitive walkthrough even before you deploy your discovery system, but it's never too late to use this evaluation method, and it can go a long way towards fixing basic problems with your system.

The following are some pitfalls to watch out for when performing heuristic evaluation and cognitive walkthroughs.

One person, one response: Both of these types of usability inspections can be done by one person, but the strength and reliability of the results will depend on the knowledge and thoroughness of that individual.

Overfixing: In an effort to be thorough, the inspector may find problems that would not be an issue for the average user.

Too much knowledge: When completing the task in the walkthrough, a librarian may complete the task in fewer steps than the average user by utilizing shortcuts like advanced searching, Boolean operators, or truncation.

Too little knowledge: In contrast, a nonlibrarian web designer may have little knowledge of patron research needs and might design a cognitive walk-through that is clunky and noneffective, and which would not ever be duplicated by a user.

Faux UX: Ultimately, neither of these methods captures the "actual" user response to the site.

Instruments

The format of the instrument(s) that you create for a usability study will vary by the type of study you conduct. You may decide to keep things simple and use a paper printout for your survey, questionnaire, list of tasks to be completed, rubric or evaluation sheet to be completed by the researcher, and examples of current web page(s) or web page prototypes. If you decide to approach your study from a more technical perspective, you can design online instruments to use with live websites or online prototypes, online polls and surveys, or tests created with usability software. You can create and code these electronic tools from scratch, or you can use free online tools like Survey-Monkey or library applications like LibGuides to create study instruments.

Polls and Surveys

This is one of the quickest and easiest ways to do usability testing. If you're working on refining a single aspect of your discovery system, you could stick with a short, simple survey for your patrons, such as "Which discovery system name would make you more likely to use the system for research: Quailsearch or Search Everything?" One of the simplest ways you can test usability is by presenting your patrons with printouts (color copies, if possible) of your design choices, such as whether they prefer pull-down menus or radio buttons or what terminology they prefer (e.g., "Books & More" vs. "Books, DVDs, CDs,"), and having them select their preferred option on the spot. This type of testing can take place anywhere—at the library service desk, in a classroom, or at a student union. In these cases, your goal is to extract a quick, knee-jerk reaction from your participants. Giving your participants extra time for contemplation will only allow them to second guess themselves.

This type of testing works best as a choice between two options only. For example, if you want participants to choose between a discovery search results page with a blue theme or a green theme, you would create mockups of both, printout quality color copies, place them side by side on the table, and ask the participant to choose their favorite image. If you have additional choices, say maybe a neutral gray theme, you can add this to the mix, but do so in combination with only one other choice. If you wanted to determine which color theme was preferred by students, you would work through your options in sets of two, keeping the winning theme in each case, until you go through the whole set. Think of this like an eye exam where you are asked to pick the clearer of two options. This kind of testing can also be used to ask participants to determine their preferred location for facets or limits on the discovery system results page and for other page design considerations.

Informal polls are another way to get quick user input on the look and feel of your discovery system, determine whether or not the users are satisfied with the discovery experience, and whether or not they have any unmet needs. Paper surveys have long been a staple in the library world, but advances in technology now permit pop-up polls to appear on websites in small windows that allow users to voice their opinion with a single mouse click. Pop-up polling software may be included with your discovery system or may be part of your website content management system. There are also numerous free software solutions available on the Internet such as SurveyMonkey and Poll Everywhere. We'll be discussing the screen capture and coding software Morae from Techsmith in the upcoming sections of this book. If you decide to use this software, keep in mind that it offers polling as a feature. Basic multiple choice and scaling polls can be created easily and placed in the study file along with the task questions.

Here are some things to consider when creating a pop-up poll:

Appearance: Make sure to include your branding or library name so that the poll comes across to the user as a legitimate questionnaire. Users are wary of advertisements designed to look like pop-up polls, and may not trust your poll unless it looks official.

Question design: The poll should be short, and each question should have a multiple choice or true/false answer. This is not the place for written answer questions. The polling software may limit the number of choices that can be offered.

Audience: Do you want or need to identify your audience? You may be able to direct specific polling questions to a particular audience if your users are given the option to self-identify (by logging in or by IP address). For example, you could target a question about advanced searching to graduate students only.

Duration: Be prepared to run your poll for a limited amount of time. There is nothing to be gained from overrunning the poll. You do not want the same individuals voting more than once and you do not want users to become annoyed with the same poll.

Sampling: Decide how many poll results it will take to give you an adequate response rate. To determine the sample size, calculate your overall use numbers for your discovery system through your analytics program and then decide what portion of that number will serve to capture the opinions of the entire group. Most polling software is capable of sending out intermittent polls to, say, every third user that accesses the page. The polls can also be programmed to stop access once a certain number of responses have been received.

Polls as PR: A pop-up poll can also be a good way to draw a user's attention to a new or little-used feature of your discovery system. For best effect, design your polling question so that it requires the user to interact with your web page or new feature. If you have been making small, iterative changes to your website or search page, a poll can draw attention to an improvement that may have otherwise gone unnoticed.

Card Sorting

Card sorting is another easy way to do basic usability testing, though it requires a little more planning and structure than a simple survey. To create a card-sorting exercise, you will need to ask your participants to meet you at a specific location, where you will present them with a series of cards labeled with terms or design options and ask them to pick the card that they prefer. For example, you could ask your participant to choose between two terms (e.g., "scholarly" vs. "peer-reviewed") in order to help you determine the best terminology to use in your discovery system, or you could design a series of cards related to menu options or links on your discovery system web pages and ask the participant put them in the location or order that makes the most sense to them. You can also use card sorting to get input on the placement of subcategories for pull-down and other menus. For example, you could create top-level categories for "Limit To" and "Source Types" and subcategory cards for "Full Text," "My Library Only," "Scholarly Journals," "Books," "News," "Magazines," and so forth, and ask the participant to put the subcategories where they best fit in the order that makes the most sense to them.

When you're administering the card-sorting instrument, keep in mind that placement of the subcategory cards on the table can influence the way the participant considers each entry.   Here are two different methods:

1. Shuffle the stack and have all the cards face down in a single pile.
2. Place every card face up and spread them out over the table so that all can be seen by the participant.

Each method has its advantages. With the upside down pile, the participant must make decisions on one subcategory at a time, and each card receives individual consideration. With the spread out, visible method, participants tend to group subcategories (either mentally or physically) before placing them under the category, attempting to find similarities within the group before considering the category terms. When taking notes on participant behavior while using the spread out method, be sure to track the subcategory cards the participant reached for first. These first cards will often be the same for multiple participants and usually indicate that the participant has a clear understanding of that subcategory terminology or that it conveys a valuable service. Likewise, take note of those cards that participants put off until the end. This delay in card selection may indicate that the participant is confused by the wording on the card (perhaps due to use of library jargon) or that the participant doesn't feel that the card fits well into any of the categories. With both methods, it is important to give the participant an option to put aside any subcategories they feel are not a good fit with the predesigned categories. When the study is finished, ask the participant if they could group any of the subcategories they put aside and/or if they could offer any suggestions for category names that would match these subcategories.

Focus Groups

A quick and easy way to get feedback on your discovery system is to pull together a focus group of users to discuss their experiences with and expectations of the discovery system. Most focus groups should be no larger than 10–12 individuals. There can be benefits to creating a mini focus group of only four to five participants, because you'll have time to get full, in-depth answers from all of your participants. While focus groups usually take place as face-to-face encounters, software is also available to facilitate online group discussions. You can design your focus group to consist of a diverse representation that spans the library's patron population, or you can have a series of focus groups with representation from only one population at a time.

Preparation for a focus group is minimal. It requires a private room with seating and a projected computer, if that is necessary. Bear in mind that you don't need to follow the televised depiction of focus groups, which often shows hidden observers behind one-way glass. This kind of focus group looks impressive, but is not necessary for library research. In addition to the participants, the focus group should include a moderator and at least one observer. Because it can be hard to be objective when you have been involved in the creation of a tool like a discovery system, it may be best to find a moderator from outside the library. In a university or college setting, you should be able to find individuals trained in meeting facilitation and mediation. In a school or public library setting, you can contact local churches and municipal offices to see if they can recommend an appropriate moderator. It will be the moderator's job to keep the session flowing and encourage participation from each individual. You may wish to video or audiotape the session. If so, this should be approved by all participants ahead of time.

The moderator needs to set the tone for the session by establishing a few basic rules:

- Stress that the library is interested in *everyone's* opinions.
- Ask that the participants be respectful and not interrupt when another is speaking.
- Ask that the participants respect each other's anonymity. Opinions given should not be repeated by anyone after leaving the room.

One of the moderator's most important jobs is to make sure that each individual has the opportunity to speak. With differing personality types, some participants will speak up right away, while others will need some time to hit their comfort zone with the group before entering the conversation. The moderator needs to be mindful of these differences and try not to let one or two participants dominate the discussion.

One way to address this problem of uneven focus group participation is to take advantage of focus group software like itracks or FocusGroupIt. To join an online focus group, the moderator and each study participant log into a chat room from their own computer at separate locations. Communicating via chat room can allow some participants to zone out and just lurk, reading the comments posted by the others, while some participants dominate the conversation. To help solve this problem, some focus group software provides a red-yellow-green light system that indicates how much text has been typed by each individual for each question asked. Participants can see the light system and are warned at the beginning of the session that they may not receive compensation for the study if their light changes from yellow to red more than once.

It would be handy if this kind of stoplight system could be used in a face-to-face setting, but there is no practical way to do this. Instead, prior to the session, the moderator may want to list all the participants' names after each question on their set of notes. During the session, the moderator can then place a tick mark after the name each time that participant speaks, in order to make sure that there was equal participation across the group. It is usually best if the focus group discussions can be free flowing, but it may be necessary at times for the moderator to prompt some participants for a response.

The focus group discussion questions should be designed to explore users' opinions, expectations, and ideas. The types of questions used should be open-ended and fairly vague, not restrictive or leading. Here are some examples:

- Have you used the library's discovery system to do research?
- If so, what did you think of it?
- What did you like best about the system?
- Can you think of any way that the system could work better for you?

You may want to show images of your discovery system interfaces or demonstrate small tasks and ask the group participants for their initial response. When creating your focus group questionnaire, be mindful of time: focus groups should meet for no longer than one or two hours, and you want to make sure that you provide enough time after each question for each participant to respond. Also, be aware that observations given following an earlier question may end up answering one further down the list. The moderator needs to be observant and flexible enough to know to skip a redundant question.

The observer should be introduced by the moderator, and their role in the proceedings should be explained and acknowledged to the participants. While the moderator asks the questions, it is the observer's job to take notes on individual comments and to also note when other participants agree or disagree. It is very important for the observer to note changes in participants' body language, as that can provide clues as to how the participant feels about a particular topic. It may be beneficial for the observer to be seated a foot or two away from the group in order to best see everyone. Unless called upon to do so, there is no need for the observer to speak or be involved in the discussion. It is important that the moderator and observer meet soon after the focus group is over in order to compare notes while the event is still fresh in their minds.

Usability Lab Studies

Another way to gather qualitative information about how your patrons are using your discovery system is to study their interactions with the discovery system on a computer in a usability lab or on a designated computer in another private place. Usability lab studies are a great way to get real data about how your patrons interact with your discovery system because you'll be able to watch and record the specific ways that your patrons use the system in order to complete the tasks that you assign them to perform.

If you're interested in getting a general overview of how your patrons are using your system, it can be useful to design an instrument that doesn't tie your participants to narrow questions. Some of the most natural results can come from vague, nonleading study questions that allow the researcher to observe the entire, often winding path to discovery. One way to get a glimpse at the way your patrons use your system is to create a scavenger hunt list of questions for your participants to complete, and then collect data about the steps that they take to find the answers. Another option is to create a free range-type search session in which the researcher gives the participants a general research question and allows the users to find their own path. Both types of searching have value and both can be done in conjunction with a variety of data collection methods.

The scavenger hunt-type search is a good way to identify significant problem areas in your discovery system, or it can be used if you want reassurance that basic resources can be easily found. The first step is to write your questions in a nonleading manner. These questions should be as specific as possible with actual titles, limits, and so forth.

Scavenger hunt question examples:
- What is the call number for *Trump: The Art of the Deal*?
- Locate one journal article on taxidermy.
- Find one newspaper article about robots written before 1960.
- Is the library's DVD of *The Color Purple* available in Blu-Ray?

When you're preparing your list of questions or tasks, remember that word choice is crucial to the success or failure of your study. Terms that are obvious to librarians are not always clear to your study population. For example, we've seen studies where the participants get bogged down by their literal interpretations of the task terms. If asked to find primary sources, they will look for a link that says "primary sources." We've also seen faculty assignments that read "find five sources that must include monographs, scholarly articles, and thesis," and when the student tries to complete the assignment, they bypass links for books, peer-reviewed articles, and doctoral works because they don't understand that these items meet the assignment criteria.

A second option for usability lab instrument design is free-range searching, where you present the participant with only one task that he or she can easily keep in mind without needing to refer back to a numbered list of questions, or review a list of prompts on the computer screen. By keeping the question vague, it allows the participant to choose his or her own path to find the answer to the question. Examples of free-range questions are:

- Find an article on organic food production and print the entire article.
- Find a book on bipolar disorder and print the citation in APA style.
- Find a definition for the musical term "staccato" in an online reference book and copy/paste it in a Word document.

When creating free-range questions, it is important to keep them unstructured by not asking the participant to use a particular title or search strategy. You also want to make the questions goal oriented by requesting a final product: a printed article, a printed citation, call number and library location of a book, a completed interlibrary loan form, and so on. There needs to be a goal so that the participant knows when they have completed the task. Asking for proof of completion in the form of a printout or a Word document makes sure that the researcher can see the entire path that the participant took to task success (or not) rather than simply a portion of the research path.

A/B Testing

Also known as "multivariate testing," "live testing," or "bucket testing," A/B testing can be used to compare how users interact with two slightly different live versions of the same web page in order to see which version is easier to use. Unlike the paper site design comparison method where users were presented with both versions of the website and were asked to choose which design they liked better, you can use A/B testing to deploy one version of the website at a time to randomly assigned groups of users for a predetermined period of time. You can use direct observation, screen capture, and/or page analytics to capture user behavior during each phase of the testing. Once you have deployed all your designs (preferably no more than two or three), you can review your data analytics to see if the page differences affected user behavior. Here are some examples of the kind of data that you can gather and compare using A/B testing:

- Length of time that the participant spent on your web pages
- How quickly they identified and used your discovery system
- Which links the participants found and followed
- Whether or not they tried to follow traditional research paths, such as going to individual databases or the classic catalog, rather than using the discovery system

A/B testing is an easy way to answer the question, "I wonder which library homepage design would work better to highlight the discovery system?" It does not involve recruiting participants, doesn't take much researcher time, and is available at little or no cost. You can design two web pages with either subtle or drastic differences. For example, you could design your pages so that the only variable would be that the A page shows the words "Find books, articles and DVDs" in gray shadowed print inside your discovery system search box, and your B page displays the same phrase in black font directly under the search box. Or, you could design the two pages to look completely different from each other, with the A page created to look like a traditional, busy library home page with the discovery search box and about 30 additional links, and the B pages designed as a white page with only the discovery search box, similar to the Google start page. Because each type of page is sent to random users at the same time, you can test more drastic looks without getting the user backlash that you might receive by presenting both sites to the same user because each user will only see one of the versions, not both. When users only receive one choice, they will tend to judge it on its own merit and give a more thorough and unbiased analysis than they will if they are given something else with which to compare it.

Your website's content management system or service provider may provide their own A/B testing platform, or you can pursue several free options on the Internet such as Google Analytics (free) or Optimizely (inexpensive). The pages that you design for this testing need to be functional pages in every way; they are not mock-ups to be printed on paper. Every link and search must be live. Each version must also have a durable URL and, depending on your A/B testing service, you may be required to use the same URL with version_1, version_2 appended at the end. Before the test is implemented, you must also define your test audience and the length of time for testing. Your audience will be a random sample of your general users unless you have methods of self-identifying built into your site or the ability to recognize certain users by IP address (i.e., users at a certain library branch or on campus vs. off campus). The length of time for the study will depend on your overall use numbers, but most studies produce reliable results in a few days to a few weeks.

Selecting a Data Collection Method

You'll need to consider how you plan to analyze the data that you collect, because that will affect your study design. Do you have access to specialized software for coding or will you be cataloging and calculating the data manually? Do you need strong statistical analysis for a formal report or to publish the findings? Do you have access to your discovery system analytics, or will you need to work with your system administrator to gather this data? You should think through to the final product at the very beginning of your study design, as well as through every step of the research process.

When working with live participants, there are many ways to collect data. You can use direct observation, screen capture recording, audio, video, and eye-tracking recording, surveying, polling, or more indirect measures like heat mapping and analytics. The method you use will largely be determined by how close you want to get to actual normal patron use. Many methods of studying usability with direct observation make it evident to the study participants that they are being observed the entire way through the process. This can lead to nonnormal, anxious behavior by the user and/or skewed positive results from "people pleasing" participants who want to make the researchers happy and who may not be honest about their normal research methods.

Direct Observation

The direct observation method usually means that the researcher sets up the research session so that they will be sitting with the participant and watching how he or she navigates the assigned tasks or answers the questions. The researcher can either type or handwrite their notes about the actions of the participant. There are several things that can simplify this process for the researcher:

Note taking: Preprint your research questions with one question to a page, leaving ample space for your notes.

Research paths: If you're watching to see the path that the user takes to meet the research goal, take the time to jot down ahead of time what you think is the most direct path to each answer and write that after each question. If the study participant successfully follows this route, all you have to do is place a checkmark in front of this description.

Track participant behavior: Make a link trail by jotting down the name of every link taken so that you can retrace the route taken by the participant.

Be aware that your participant will likely work through the research questions very quickly, and it will be necessary to use a type of shorthand to describe the process. For that reason, after the participant leaves, immediately go back through your notes and write a longer description of the study results, as you may not understand your scribbled remarks after a few days.

Direct observation is one of the quickest and least technical ways to capture data about participant behavior, but remember that the presence of the researcher in the room can possibly change the way that the participant completes his or her tasks. Another drawback to direct observation is that it can be hard to keep up with taking notes on the actions of the participants, and you might miss crucial research behavior. You might also only focus on the parts of the process in which you're especially interested, rather than capturing all the steps that the participant took in order to complete the tasks.

Screen Capture Recording

A more efficient, less invasive way to capture participant research behavior is to use screen capture technology to record their mouse movements on the screen as they work through the research tasks and questions. Screen capture technology records the actions of the participant and preserves their anonymity, unlike video or audio recording. There are many flavors of screen capture software on the market, some of which you may already have at your library for use on other projects. Software like Camtasia, often used by libraries to create tutorials, can be used to record research sessions. Free software like Techsmith's Jing can also be used for sessions lasting less than five minutes. Higher end screen capture software such as Techsmith's Morae is also available, though the cost may be out of reach for most libraries.

Any one of the screen capture software products listed above can provide you with good enough video quality to determine how your participants interact with your discovery system. However, you'll need to consider the size of the finished video when you're setting up your tasks and research questions. Depending on the type of computer that you're using and your amount of free file space, you may need to limit the number of tasks that you ask the participant to perform in order to keep the size of the resulting video manageable. One way to decrease the file size is by limiting the frame of the screen that you'd like to record. The smaller the screen size, the smaller the resulting file. Most screen capture software allows the user to select the recording window size in pixels or inches. Some of them will also allow the window to follow the cursor as the mouse is moved, but note that if you choose this option, it makes that recording harder to follow during the data analysis phase because you'll lose your frame of reference. However, since you're already familiar with the discovery search interface, it may not be necessary for you to see the full screen. Although a minor concern, choosing this mouse-tracking option can sometimes cause the reviewer to feel motion sickness while reviewing the data, because of the often jerky, stop and start motions made by the participant.

As noted above, screen capture software is less intrusive to the participant than having the researcher sitting in the same room and taking notes. Most screen capture software has a subtle screen presence when it is running. It is usually either invisible or has a dotted-line frame when filming. Screen capture will record everything typed, scanned, and clicked on while the study is taking place. It also records in real time, which gives the researcher insight into how long a particular task takes for each participant. When the participant is finished, the screen capture video is saved and can be reviewed at the researcher's convenience.

One interesting option provided by the Morae software is the ability to capture each research question as a separate task. When the participant accesses the study on the computer, screen capture recording begins immediately and the first question appears at the top of the computer screen. The participant must click on a start task button at the beginning and an end task button when they have found the answer, at which point the second task appears on the screen. This method forces the participant to concentrate on one question at a time and does not permit them to jump ahead and skip questions, which can help improve the consistency of your data and results.

Audio Recording, Video Recording, and Eye Tracking

When you're looking for more information than you can glean from mere observation, you have several options. Audio recording of a participant's spoken observations, video recording of their facial expressions and mannerisms, and tracking of their eye movements as they search the computer screen are all viable research methods. Using one or more of these tools during your usability study can greatly increase your understanding of your users' overall experience. This type of extra exploration can answer many of the "whys" and "hows" that are often left lingering after a basic usability test. The downside to this type of testing is that it may be more difficult to find users willing to participate, it can be expensive and time consuming for the researchers to set up and monitor, and it will require additional hours to analyze the resulting data.

Software like Techsmith's Morae provides these additional observational options. If a web camera is affixed to the computer, the researcher can opt to video record the user's facial expressions or track their eye motion as it scans the screen. The software also provides an audio option to record participant speech, which can be used to capture the participant's train of thought as they respond to each question. Train of thought recording, in conjunction with screen capture, gives you more information than screen capture alone because it can help you identify not only the link that the participant selected, but also why he or she did not follow the other available paths.

Not every participant will be comfortable with being video recorded or with talking through their research steps and decisions for an audio recording. Some personality types are more naturally attuned to this kind of research, and for those who are disinclined to share their thoughts, constant coaxing does not usually make them more interested in doing so. Be aware that not everyone will respond enthusiastically to being recorded. However, active, verbal participants can provide you with great insights that cannot be acquired by watching user actions alone.

One of the most enlightening things to be learned from an active verbal participant is why a particular information path was not taken or even considered. Most often, the audio responses indicate that a route wasn't taken because of past experience on the site or that some link text was so vague that they were not sure where it would lead them. We often forget that the general public does not have the natural curiosity of the average librarian, and a vague or misleading term can lead to that link being ignored by the participant. It can be heartbreaking for the researcher to hear a study participant orally recite a list of links that a committee spent hours crafting, only to hear them say repeatedly "I don't know what that means" after each term.

Audio recording is also a good way to discover new, viable information routes on your discovery site. Once librarians find an information route that works, it is hard for them to see all the other routes that a first time user might use. It is by listening to the sound, logical musings of our users as they try to click on links that are doomed to dead end that makes us realize the frustrating walls that we can unintentionally set up. An example of this kind of dead end would be a link marked "more . . ." that the user assumes will take him/her to the full text of an article, but only supplies an additional sentence or two of the abstract.

THE RABBIT HOLE

True frustration is watching a patron choose a link that removes them from the discovery system and then watching them attempt a search that would have worked had they stayed where they were. For example, your discovery system can be designed so that a list of recommended databases appears near the top of the search results screen. To a veteran researcher, these suggested databases are a helpful reminder that there are other, more targeted research options if their initial discovery system search did not give them the type of results that they wanted. Librarians assume that novice users will simply ignore these links and scroll down to look at the results of their search, but this is not always the case. The extra database links might look like the next step in the research process to a new user, and if he or she clicks on the link, it will take them away from retrieved citations on the results list and leaves them staring at a blank search page. Listening to a user trying to talk themselves back to the discovery search can leave the researcher feeling demoralized and helpless. This is further frustrated by well-meaning design that opens new resources in new windows, thus making the back arrow key ineffective. Even more than one window open can throw off many users.

Indirect Observation

Heat Mapping

One of the most interesting ways to get a true sense of how our users interact with the whole screen space of a web page is by using a heat mapping service. Heat mapping results look like the film footage from military night maneuvers: the dark background shows the outlines of people and animals glowing in a rainbow of colors, ranging from blue on the outside blending into yellows, oranges, and bright red for the internal organs. Usability heat mapping of web pages works much the same way. The results you receive show a black, X-ray-type film overlay on top of your web page. A layout of colored dots represents the number of user clicks on your page. Blue dots apply to the least frequently clicked page areas, green, yellow, and orange represent increased usage, and red dots show up like bull's-eyes to highlight the areas with greatest use. Heat map testing is an ideal way to analyze library website and discovery system usage because it captures the natural use of the pages by all users without any intervention or possible influence from the researcher.

Heat mapping is available as a subscription service, and the most recognized provider is a company called Crazy Egg, which can be commissioned for a one-time study, or it can be set up with an annual account for continuous usability use. The pricing reflects the number of pages you want to track, with the price increasing with the number of pages selected. Although you need to pick a specific number of pages for your subscription, the URLs of the pages that you test are not set in stone, and you can change them as often as you like in order to get a better overview of how your entire discovery system and library site are being used. Bear in mind that heat map testing is only available for web pages with persistent URLs, so it is not an option for pages whose URLs are dynamically generated, such as discovery system search results pages.

When submitting a web page for heat map testing, you need to determine the duration of data collection time needed for a good overall sampling of patron usage. This decision is easier if you have a general sense of the average site usage. For a very busy website, one week of results may be sufficient, but for others, a month or three months may give a better indication of how your patrons interact with your site. It can also be useful to be strategic when choosing the date range for your heat mapping. For example, in an academic library, you may want to set the collection time for a busy week in the middle of your fall or spring semester instead of choosing a week in the summer, when students are less likely to use your site. Public libraries may want to track usage both during the summer and also when the local schools are back in session.

Heat mapping can give you an immediate and visual indication as to whether or not your patrons are invested in your discovery system, or if they're still relying heavily on your traditional databases and OPAC. If all these resources reside on the same web page, heat mapping can provide clear evidence as to whether or not patrons are using your discovery system. A good test would be to turn on heat mapping for one week and then repeat for the same time period every two months. This should give you a clear picture if your discovery system is gaining acceptance over time. Do your database or classic catalog links show up consistently as red in the heat map, but your discovery system is blue or not highlighted at all? If so, then it's time to consider what you can do to improve your discovery system's accessibility, instruction in library classes, buy-in from campus faculty, and general PR.

Here is a true-life example of heat mapping that demonstrates a user need that was not being met. Years of web use have trained us to believe that rectangular images are clickable buttons. A university library did not take this into account when designing its live reference chat window. The web page was coded to show a green rectangle jpeg image with the words "Librarian available" when the site was staffed and a red rectangle marked "Librarian not available" when it was unstaffed. A heat map of the web page showed a strong red dot over the unlinked "Librarian not available" red rectangle. It appears that a fair number of users not only mistook the image for a button, but also thought it was some sort of doorbell that could magically make a librarian appear!

Heat mapping can bring up some interesting results. Often, the results will prove the 80/20 rule of web design, with only 20 percent of your linked items receiving 80 percent of the hits to your site. It can be disconcerting to see that many links receive few or zero clicks even over a month-long period. Along with showing you whether or not your patrons use your discovery system, the heat mapping can also show you how your patrons choose to fine-tune their searches. You might find that your full text only limiter will often appear as bright red (extremely popular) and your advanced search limit may be colorless, as if it wasn't even linked.

One of the most fascinating results from heat mapping can be the realization that users click on text or images that are not linked, such as your discovery system logo. Users might think that the branding image is equivalent to a "Search" button to activate the search term they entered in the search box, or that it is the way to get into the system to start a search. Do not take these results lightly—our users are telling you what they expect to find. If you get these kinds of results from your heat mapping study, you'll need to make every effort to improve these areas and make these images or text link to another page or service, if at all possible.

Your heat mapping results can give you concrete data to help you modify and simplify your library website and discovery system in order to make it easier for your patrons to use. If your heat mapping data shows you that your classic catalog or databases are not being used very often, you could make their links less prominent by decreasing their font size or changing their location, or you may decide to remove from the web page. The beautiful thing about heat mapping data is that it's nonbiased and wasn't swayed by any researcher interaction. It's a clear, true portrayal of how patrons are using your site, and it's a great tool to use when trying to convince your colleagues that changes to your web design are necessary. Librarians are often more resistant to change than our patrons, and it can be a hard sell to get them to agree to moving or removing links to traditional research tools like the OPAC or specific databases.

Analytics

Most discovery systems offer an analytics component, but the depth and detail of the analytics may vary, depending on your vendor. Analytics provide impersonal, behind-the-scenes raw data about search types, search terms, usage patterns, and click rates which can fill in gaps and round out the big picture of your discovery system usage. It may be helpful to think of analytics as giving you a snapshot of the "herd mentality" usage of the site vs. the more personal, one-on-one usability observation. Analytics give you quantitative data to further support your qualitative observational findings, and they answer questions like:

- Where are our users coming from?
- How long did they stay on the site?
- How many links did they click while they were on the site?
- What search terms did they enter?

Traffic or visitor statistics are a basic component of most analytics products, and they give you a sense of who is using your site and how often. A visitor is not necessarily the same as an individual because the program is determining a visitor by the IP address, and there could be an entire group of individuals conducting the search from one computer. The IP address works as the fingerprint for one exact location. Here are some things to keep in mind about visitor data:

- It's collected for a specific time period and the visitor criteria (new, repeat, return, unique) are only relevant for that time period.
- A new or unique visitor is one that has entered the site during the collection period at least once.
- The unique visitor count gives you the total number of entries from each individual IP address.
- Repeat visitors connect with the site two or more times within the collection period.
- Return visitors are those whose IP address appears in multiple studies, which can be determined by comparing IP addresses between studies.

These types of visitor statistics are the most common analytics tools and can be used to show popularity and use of individual web pages in a discovery system.

Analytics can be used to track the search terms that your patrons enter in your discovery system search box, which can give you insight into the kind of searching that your patrons are doing. For example, if your patrons are looking for the names of specific databases, then they may not understand that they can limit their discovery search results to the database provider required by their professor (e.g., JSTOR), or your website may not be designed so that they can figure out how to go to individual databases directly. Are your patrons using whole language searching? If so, then maybe you need to spend more time in instruction sessions teaching them how to use the discovery system's advanced search. Search term lists only tell you what was searched, not what was found, but that list can give you insight into the kinds of things your patrons expect to find in the discovery system. The search terms list ranks the terms most often searched, and it can also easily identify whole language searching and citation searches.

Some enterprising librarians have also found ways to manipulate the analytics codes in the discovery system programs to allow for further investigation into areas clicked after the search term results were revealed. Some discovery systems, such as EBSCO's EDS, are starting to offer the ability to integrate Google Analytics code into your site pages, which can facilitate even greater analytic collections for your site. Advanced analytics can give us further insight into how our patrons are interacting with aspects of the discovery system beyond the initial search, and can answer questions such as:

- What percentage of patrons select an article immediately from the results list after searching (implying that they found a useful source on their first search)?
- What percentage of the patrons go to the limits and filters in your system after they do a search? If many patrons do this, maybe you should adjust your web design to let your patrons start at the advanced search screen rather than the basic search screen, or add filters as an option to your homepage discovery system search box.
- How do patrons get to the full text from a search results list? By using the result title? By clicking on a pdf or html link?
- How often are patrons using your link resolvers or Interlibrary Loan links to find full text?

Analytics give you the opportunity to identify all the ways that your users get to your discovery search, and the numbers and percentages of patrons who use each entry point. This analytics feature can often be eye opening, and can show you whether or not your library web pages lead your patrons to your discovery system as easily as you think they do. Librarians tend to use the access methods that we designed to be the starting points for discovery—it's common for us to have saved a direct URL to the site as either our browser homepage or, at the very least, a bookmark. Analytics results can show you the number of users entering with a direct URL, entering from a search engine search or coming in via a link or your library page or from any number of other websites.

Your analytics package will give you referrer statistics, which is the term for the web page from which the contact with the discovery system originated. The different types of referrers are:

Internal referrers: These come from within your own website such as a link from a web page on your site or a Research Guide link to your discovery system.
External referrer: This comes from outside of your site such as a link in a Blackboard or Moodle faculty web page or a LibGuide page.
Search referrer: These come from results from searches in a web search engine like Google or Bing.

These statistics can give you a better idea of where your discovery links are most visible for patrons and where they're most easily accessed. This information can help you identify and enhance locations on your web pages where your discovery system presence isn't working as well as you'd like it to work.

Your analytics package can help you determine which pieces of your discovery system web page structure are getting the most hits from patrons. It's important to understand the terms that the analytics package uses to describe the areas of your site. The "entry page" is the first page the user enters on your website. You will likely have multiple entry pages listed on an analytics report.

The entry page should not be confused with the landing page. The landing page is the web page you have designated as the *preferred* starting point for your discovery system. In some cases, your landing page may be a basic Google search–type page that is sparse on content and mostly consists of a long search box and a little bit of site branding. Your landing page could also be your main library web page, which you may have designed to feature a prominent search box for the discovery system. It is important to note that a landing page is something that you designate, but an entry page is determined by the search behavior of your users. A landing page can and should appear on your list of entry pages, but only one entry page will be your landing page. To improve the number of users entering on your landing page, be sure to promote it in your PR and instruction.

Your analytics report will also list your users' exit pages, or the last known location for a user on your site. Analysis of exit pages can show if users are following through on finding full-text of eBooks and articles, or they can also indicate if the user got stuck on a 404 or broken link web page. Entry pages and exit pages are time stamped. Subtracting the entry time from the exit time gives you the visit duration. Analyzing the content of exit pages in coordination with visit duration times can provide some indication of user success and user satisfaction.

Your analytics results may surprise you, and not in a good way. You may find that your patrons use a wide variety of entry pages and relatively few find the landing page that you worked hard to design and promote. It is a worthwhile exercise to enter your site through each entry page and reenact the user's journey. Note which entry pages require the greatest number of clicked links to get to the landing page. Take the time to collect duration times for those users. Were the times excessively long as they muddled through the discovery system research process? Or, were the durations extremely short because the patrons gave up and quickly exited the system?

Creating Consent Forms

Once you've designed your instrument and selected your data collection method, your next step is to create your consent form. Asking participants to sign a consent form is a good policy regardless of the type of library in which you work. The form can be distributed to your participants on paper or online. The essential parts of a consent form are:

- The participant's name
- Date
- A brief description of the study stating the purpose and duration
- A statement granting the reviewer permission to use the data collected

Be specific on any possible use of the data, and err on the side of including all possible outlets where your data might be displayed. Study results may be published in academic journals and books, video clips may be included in commercials or tutorials, direct quotes may be used in PR materials, and data may be used in future studies.

Consent is especially important when surveying or studying children, defined here as anyone under the age of 18. If you are working with a younger population, be sure that your consent form has a place for the child's name, the parent's name, and the parent's signature. Remember that even in academic settings there can be students under the age of 18, and it can often be difficult to obtain a parental signature because the students may be attending college far from home. For this reason, it may be practical to limit your study to students over the age of 18. It's a good idea to make the participant's age one of your first questions when interviewing potential participants.

Seeking Permission for the Study

Your next step is to request permission to conduct the usability study from the IRB at your institution or your governing body. Be prepared to submit a very detailed plan of your study, along with any study-related documentation or files. The ultimate goal of any review board is to protect the study participants and the integrity of the institution. The IRB can sometimes help you by finding flaws in your plans or by suggesting more practical ways to conduct your research. An IRB review is often required before you can submit your findings for publication in scholarly journals or other outlets.

One question that is frequently asked in official reviews of usability instruments is if any deception will take place during the testing. While librarianship is usually applauded for its transparency, there are times when it is OK to deceive. For example, you could add a silly or nonsense choice to a multiple choice answer on a survey to make sure that users are taking it seriously. Another bit of deception could be to purposely misspell a word in the title you have asked the participant to find in order to see if they will click on a "did you mean" option or bother to scan down a results list if the title doesn't appear as the first hit.

Another form of deception is one for the sake of the environment. A good way to test whether or not a participant has completed a task like "find an article that meets these criteria" or "find the full-text of an article," is to ask them to print the article. The researcher will have no need for these printouts except to use them as proof of task completion, and it's a waste of paper and resources to have the print jobs go through the printer. With a little bit of technology tweaking, you can set up your printer settings to print to a phantom (nonexistent) printer without sending an error message to the user. This allows the researcher to easily be able to identify that the user has selected "print" without wasting trees on chapters and articles that neither the researcher nor the participant intend to read.

Recruiting Participants

Recruiting participants for your study can take many forms:

- Approaching the individual in person and asking, "Do you have a few minutes . . ."
- E-mail recruitment to either an entire population or a subset of that population
- Web page, blog, social media, or other online recruitment
- Library signage asking for volunteers

Your recruitment strategy selection will be dependent on your target audience and your prior knowledge of the best methods for reaching that population.

If you are looking for first-time visitors and newbies to your library and your resources, you may want to recruit from First-Year Experience courses at the college level or at the beginning of a summer reading program at a public library. If there are specific age or experience limitations, start your advertising with a lead-in that reads something like, "Are you a library patron over the age of 18?" or "Are you new to our library (have visited fewer than four times)?" Simply posting a sign with one of these lead-ins can pull in willing participants, and this is important, you do want them to be willing.

Formal sampling methods were discussed in the section on determining the size of your sample. Another way to recruit participants is by using volunteer sampling, which is when an invitation is extended to a large group and the participants self-select if they would like to participate. This type of sampling can be broad or narrowly targeted. For example, you can contact all university students regardless of age or class ranking, or you can contact students of a particular age or majoring in a specific subject. To attract participants from a particular target population, you may need to get creative with your recruiting. To locate students in a specific major, you may want to focus on 300- and 400-level courses in that subject area. Ask the instructor if you can have a few minutes of class time to offer a personal invitation to their students to participate in your study. If you are looking for non-library user volunteers for a study or focus group, you will need to go outside the library to advertise. You can go hi-tech and advertise on non-library social media sites run by other members of your community, or go low-tech by placing posters advertising for study participants in locations where people are typically bored and will read anything, such as a health center waiting room and laundry rooms in dorms.

Whether potential participants are approached in person or they respond to an advertisement, each person should be given a full description of the study before you assess whether or not they will meet your participant requirements. This description should include details of the study including:

- Any age, experience, or other demographic requirements
- The maximum time commitment needed for completion
- If the study will take place by casual drop-in or by appointment with the researcher
- Any risks involved
- Any incentives offered for participation
- Contact names and phone numbers of the researcher(s)
- Documented approval for the study by any governing bodies (IRB, school administration, library board)

It is common to offer an incentive to the participants, but it is not always a necessity. Many library users are more than willing to spend a few minutes helping the library, in gratitude for all they receive from it. Incentives can be as simple as a bookmark or as elaborate as merchandise gift cards, cash, or a chance to win a large gift in a lottery of study participants. It would be nice to think that your patrons would volunteer to help you do usability testing out of the goodness of their hearts, but the reality is that people are busy, and it might take a $5 gift card to convince them to share their opinions with you. On the flip side, be aware that if you do offer an incentive, even a small one, your participants' hearts may not be fully invested in your study, and they may only want the reward. You can usually identify these types of participants by the speed with which they breeze through your study questions or by the limited responses that they offer during a focus group.

The size and type of incentive should be in proportion to the commitment of time and effort asked of the individual. (There is a reason why large monetary amounts are offered for participation in studies in other fields that require taking multiple blood samples.) It should be stated ahead of time if a participant will receive the incentive even if it becomes clear after they start the study that they did not meet the participant criteria, or if they need to remove themselves from the study partway through it.

Cash and gift card incentives bring with them a different set of considerations for the research team than, say, a bookmark:

Obtaining funds and purchase: Where will the initial funding come from and who will make the purchase?

Storage: All the study sessions are seldom conducted within the same day. Where will the cash/gift cards be stored before and during the study?

Authority: Who will have access to the cash/gift cards? Who will have the authority to distribute the incentive to the participants?

Accountability: Participants should be asked to sign (in person or electronically) that they have received the incentive at the time it was given. You do not want a situation where an individual claims they participated but were not given the promised incentive. It is also important that you keep paperwork for each incentive in order to meet your organization's accounting requirements.

If your incentive is a chance at a bigger prize, make sure that your initial documentation clearly indicates that participation does not guarantee receipt of the prize. Also, collect adequate contact information from the participant (phone number, e-mail address), and inform participants approximately when the study will end and when they will be notified if they won the grand prize. This sounds obvious, but make sure that the e-mail address that they give you is one that they check regularly, as it can sometimes be difficult to communicate with participants. Or, if they give you their cell phone number, ask if they prefer a text to communicate or a voicemail.

An easy way to select the winner after the study is complete is to write each participant's name on a slip of paper, place the slips in a hat or basket, and ask a colleague to pick a slip from the container. It is a good idea to pull the slip of paper in front of a witness in case the legitimacy of the selection is questioned. Contact not only the winner, but also all participants to inform them that the raffle has concluded and a winner was selected. Due to confidentiality reasons, you will not want to disclose the winner's name. It is also a good idea to check your local tax laws, as the winner may have to declare it and pay taxes on it, depending on the cost of the item.

Recruitment and incentives considerations:

Staff participation: Even if your goal is to recruit frequent library users, it is not a good idea to recruit library workers, work-study students, or friends of the library. These people tend to be "superusers," with a strong library bias and better-than-average search abilities, and may not give you a good look at how the average user will interact with your discovery system.

Recruiting in the classroom: If you teach a credit course at a college or university, your current students may seem like the ideal "captive audience" or potential study participants. The problem is that they are "captive" and may feel that refusing participation will be reflected in their course grade. For this reason, they do not fall into the category of "willing participants."

No family members: The fine print of almost any contest or product giveaway usually includes "Company employees and family members of employees are ineligible to participate and receive prizes." This should also be your motto when offering incentives for a study, so that your study can remain clean and ethical.

Incentive funding questions: Be prepared to answer questions about the funding for study incentives. If the incentives were funded by a grant or donated by individual companies, be sure to note that in the study description given to participants. Patron concern about money spent on incentives can happen in any library, but it can be particularly damaging for a public library that might be in the midst of conducting a fundraising campaign for a different purpose. Optics matter.

Anonymity: Library usability testing usually doesn't require individuals to divulge any embarrassing personal information, but it is often easier to attract participants if they know that their responses will remain anonymous. All your assurances of anonymity will be met with raised eyebrows if you then turn around and ask for their name and e-mail address for a raffle or ask them to sign a paper stating that they received a gift card. Be prepared to reassure participants that their names will in no way be associated with the results they supply for the study, and that personal information will be destroyed after a certain length of time.

Planning Research Session Details

Before you meet with your participants, you'll need to determine where you'll meet, which research team members will conduct the study, and where you'll keep the resulting data. If you're conducting online analysis of analytics or heat maps, this will be an easy task because usually only one or two people will be involved in the data collection and analysis. However, if you're going to be working with live participants, you'll need to iron out the details of who'll interact with the subjects and where they'll meet. If you plan to conduct a paper survey at service desk locations, you'll need to make sure that all of the people who staff those desks, from librarians to clerks to student employees or pages or volunteers, are fully informed about the study purpose and best practices for conducting the study. If you're going to run a focus group with multiple moderators and observers, you need to make sure that everyone receives the same training and background information, so that the data that you collect is consistent and untainted by accidental administrative inconsistencies.

If you need a usability lab or focus group meeting location, you'll need to get all the details about those locations worked out before setting up your participant meetings. It's possible that your room may be scheduled for other events, so be sure to check reservations schedules and make sure that you submit your reservation requests well in advance of your planned meetings. If you're planning a large focus group, make sure that you reserve a big enough room, and also be sure to plan for any extra equipment that you might need, such as a computer or recording devices or other technological needs.

Take some time to consider where your study results will be stored. If you're conducting a paper survey over a period of days, where will you store the results until you're ready to review them? Will you pick them up after every shift? If you're doing some kind of online study, do you have enough data storage space to collect and hold all your study responses? How will you guarantee the privacy of your data? It's much better to plan for these details ahead of time than to get halfway through a study and realize that the meeting room that you were planning to use for your second focus group is now booked, or that you've run out of storage space on your computer and can't conduct any more screen capture sessions.

Conducting Testing

Once you have all your session details worked out, it's time to conduct your study testing. If you are meeting with live participants, here are some things to remember during your research session:

- Make sure to meet your participants at the time assigned to them.
- If you're conducting the session in an office or other staff area, make sure that there is no private information available for your participant to see, such as another patron's library account information, your personal login information for a staff computer, personal web pages, and so forth.
- Make sure that your participant understands that he or she can end the research session at any point if they become uncomfortable or need to leave.
- If you are conducting your session using screen capture or audio or video capture without a researcher present in the study room, be sure to remain available outside the room so that your participant can ask you questions if they need to do so.
- Reassure users that there is not a time limit. Participants often feel the need to apologize for "taking too long."

Following these rules of thumb will help your participants feel comfortable during their research session, and will encourage them to focus on their participation and give you honest responses to your research questions.

Collecting Data

If you're using vendor analytics or other online sources of data, it's relatively easy to go in and collect the data that you need for your study. Make sure to be consistent and compare apples to apples if you're looking at discovery system performance and user interaction over time. If you're taking a more traditional approach to data collection, such as working with paper questionnaires and surveys, make sure to stay organized and keep all your results in the same place. If you're doing something, like a card sorting exercise with participants, consider using technology like a smartphone or tablet camera to collect data about how the participants organized the cards, and then make sure to store the photos in the same place, sorted by date. Make sure that all the people helping you with the study know where to store their results, and be sure to keep track of where the data came from and when it was captured.

Data Analysis

The end results from data collection can be as simple as a paper sheet of tick marks showing the number of participants that completed a task, a pile of print surveys, printouts of database analytics compiled by the software source, physical audio or video tapes from interviews or focus groups, or audio, video, or data files housed on a PC or server. Not coincidentally, there can also be a wide range in the amount and type of data analysis needed. Manual analysis can include tallying tick marks and categorizing written observations, Excel and statistical software can help with calculations, and coding software will allow you to mark and tabulate screen capture, video, and audio recordings.

Manual Analysis

Manual analysis is the most basic form of data compilation and doesn't require any technology greater than perhaps a calculator. This type of analysis requires you to review participant feedback and draw conclusions. Your results upon review may include numeric data like percentages or averages, or may just be a summary of patron comments or researcher observations. It is usually helpful to correlate and organize your data by noting similarities and outliers. One of the benefits of using screen capture rather than taking physical notes during a direct observation session is that you can stop and rewind the screen capture video at any point while you review your data.

Microsoft Excel and Other Statistical Software Packages

If more advanced analysis is needed, you may want to invest in Microsoft Excel, Minitab, SAS, SPSS Statistics, or another software package. These packages will allow you to enter data in a spreadsheet format in numeric or textual characters, calculate with formulas, and create presentation-ready tables and charts. In addition to these features, some of these products will also assist in helping to "clean up" data before running calculations—they provide metadata features for data documentation, and they can predict outcomes beyond the results of the data entered.

Coding

Coding is a way of identifying consistencies and inconsistencies in user research behavior. You can code your data manually and track where the codes appear. Or, if you're lucky enough to have a software package like StudioCode at your institution, you can automate this process. StudioCode is a software package that was initially used to code live action video of professional sports teams, but also works for coding screen capture video, as it provides the tools for marking any interaction on the screen. If you use this software for your research, you can decide what actions you want to track before you start collecting data. For example, do you want to note every time the participant clicks on your link resolver to get the full text of an article? Do you want to mark whenever they scroll down past the first screen of results or when they click on the next page? Do you want to track how quickly they find your discovery system search box? You can create a button to track any of these actions or events.

You can also add buttons after the fact, but it's better to get a good idea of your research questions before you collect your data rather than after. Having to go back and review data after the initial collection usually leads to rushing and a focus on a few factors instead of looking at how those factors fall in the big picture. However, some fields can only be determined after observing several or all the videos one time. For example, you might notice that your participants scroll down your web page looking for the answer to your research question when it is apparent without scrolling. After noticing this behavior in more than one session, you might want to go back and track how many students take this action in each session. You might also want to add a new button when a participant takes a research path that you didn't anticipate when designing your initial coding buttons so that you can track the behavior in that session and mark it if it happens in others.

You can assign a color to each field so that it can be easily identified for various types of analysis. For example, all your search-related fields could be different shades of green, all your timing fields could be shades of red, and so on. You can also create shortcut keys (F1–F12, Ctrl+B) to make coding easier. Button fields can also be made to look like an actual object (i.e., a survey form, a computer screen), with hidden button fields under the graphic. This allows you to click on the image, effectively mirroring the actions that occur on the video and saving the time and thought process required to locate the correctly named button.

StudioCode allows the researcher to add a timeline feature to the video so that the reviewer can watch the video and click on buttons to mark the exact time each event takes place. You can also mark the beginning and end times for each action, which will let you track how long it took a participant to complete a particular task. Each button has its own line on the timeline, and these timelines can be compared across multiple participant sessions. The software will let you compare lengths of time for activities between the participants, how many times events happened, average and mean times for each actions, and so forth. Morae provides a variety of charts and graphs for your data, and you can copy and paste these images into presentation software without having to recreate them using Excel or another chart/graph tool.

Report Findings

Now that you've designed your study and collected and analyzed your data, it's time to share your results with the people who can do something about the problems you've found. It's also a good idea to disseminate your positive results, in order to share the ways in which your system is working, so that you can encourage your library staff to keep up the good work of promoting the discovery system. Depending on your organization, you may be the only person in charge of creating the discovery site, performing usability testing, and using your usability results to edit the site. Or, you may be the sole person responsible for usability testing in a larger organization, or part of a committee or team conducting usability testing, or simply a librarian who's concerned about the usability of your system. Regardless of the size or configuration of your library, you and your usability team should produce some kind of summary statement to document your findings and to aid in future planning for your discovery installation.

What's the best way to disseminate your findings? Traditional typed reports are often not the best form of presentation for usability test results. Usability results need to show patron research behavior processes, research paths taken, and buttons and links that your participants clicked. There is a lot of action to capture and words just do not do it justice. Luckily, we're living in a time where Infographics are popular, widespread, and easier to create than they were in the past. Canva and Piktochart are two free websites that you can use to create professional-looking images and charts by using simple "drag and drop" actions.

What data should you include? Most discovery system usability testing is task driven, and task completion time is a common way to show discovery system success because it's assumed that the easier the system is to use, the more quickly and efficiently the study participant will be able to complete an assigned task. One way to analyze task time is to use the traditional statistical method of finding the mean and median times, but these numbers tell the uninformed viewer very little about the test results and may even leave them in doubt about the success or failure of the task participants. A more comprehensive and visually appealing approach is to depict the range of task completion times in a chart or appealing graphic. Showing that task completion time ranged from 1 minute 20 seconds to 6 minutes 40 seconds says more to the viewer than that the median time was 3 minutes 8 seconds. Another display option would be to create a scatter chart showing the time placement of all participants over the entire range.

Participant research paths and processes are also easier to demonstrate as visual representations than with a dry written report. It can be difficult to quantify the exact ways that your patrons interact with your discovery system without using pictures. In many cases, your participants will have tried multiple link paths and experienced more than one false start before they could complete their assigned tasks. Screenshot images can be the best way to represent the various paths taken by your study participants. Screenshot capture software applications like Microsoft's Snipping Tool and Apple's command-driven screen copying are easy to use and widely available. To create a visual of the user path, start by bringing up the web page to be captured, turn on the screen capture function, use the crosshairs to define the area of the snapshot, and save the file. Some screen capture functions will then give you options to add text, shapes, and colors. You can also modify the screenshot using Microsoft Word or PowerPoint by adding word clouds and arrows to show all the paths taken by your study group and the percentage of participants that chose each path. To portray a complete path, take a screenshot of each web page opened during task completion and join them with arrows, making a kind of research storyboard.

Some user research paths can be so unexpected or illogical that they require a live demonstration for your peers and administration, or other people who are interested in your study results. If you used screen capture video as a data collection method, you can edit the video to display only the footage from that one task. If you were unable to capture the participant's search path electronically but took notes during his or her session, you can use screen capture software to record a recreation of the search. These video clips can be saved to a computer or server and shown in a live presentation or can be included as a URL in order to provide documentation for a usability results report.

One of the most important things to address in your report is suggestions for improvement or for further testing. The purpose of usability testing is to find out where you may have inadvertently created roadblocks for your patrons in their research process, and then use your study results to make your discovery system more visible, efficient, and easier for your patrons to use. Even if you were only charged with conducting the usability study and not with solving all the problems that you find, your first-hand observation of user interaction with the library's resources will most likely have sparked many ideas for improvements for your site. By adding your suggestions to the report, you can provide a starting point for those staff members who are responsible for monitoring and revising the discovery system's design and features.

Instrument and Data Retention

Now that you have collected your data, how long should you hold onto it? Is there even a need to keep it? If your results are to be published or presented, there are several reasons why it's a good idea to archive all your research-related documentation. You may want to do follow-up studies based on your previous research, other researchers might want to use your instruments and findings as a place to start their own research, or you might need to review your findings in response to questions from your print readers or in-person audience.

Here are some things to think about when deciding how long to keep your research data:

IRB requirements: Did you receive approval from an IRB or administrative body? If so, the details for using, storing, and destroying data were probably clearly outlined, and you will need to comply with the requirements of the approving body. A stipulation that data must be stored in a password-protected location and destroyed after 5 years is not unusual.

Privacy: Did you guarantee anonymity for your study participants? Can the data collected be traced back to any of them in any way? If it can't, the need for security and destruction of records is less critical than in cases where you agreed to protect the privacy of your participants. If your participants can be clearly identified, be sure to clarify which researchers are allowed access to the data and if security is adequate so that the participants' personal information is not compromised. If you decide to discard any identifying information about your participant, you should consider whether or not there is any possibility that you would need to follow-up with these individuals in future studies.

Format: In cases of surveys and polls, if the data has been cataloged, calculated, analyzed, or summarized, and there is no identifying information about the participants, there is probably little need to keep the individual paper or digital evidence.

Future studies: Have you wrung every last bit of usable data out of these results? When preparing your results for publication or presentation, you may find that you are concentrating on a few findings and largely ignoring others. You may have designed your study to cover larger research questions than you have the time or means to distill for a short presentation or paper, but you might have a need for some of the more obscure findings in the future. Before discarding research results, make sure that you are not going to regret losing that data at some future point.

Storage Methods for Study Instruments and Results

If you decide to keep your study materials, you'll need to consider the best means for storage. Paper data, such as participant surveys or questionnaires, reviewer notes, final reports, and charts/graphs, are fragile and susceptible to many possible calamities brought on by man or nature (e.g., floods, fire, accidental disposal, etc.). Paper-format objects should be kept in a clean, dry location protected from both the outside elements and from internal potential hazards like leaking pipes. If your content is meant to be kept indefinitely, it would be useful to review archival best practices for paper storage. If possible, duplicate the paper items and keep one set in a separate location. Duplication can take the form of photocopying, or scanning to produce a digital copy. If security is a concern for your materials, you can satisfy this requirement by placing the content in a locked room or filing cabinet.

Digital files, like online surveys or polls, screen capture video, audio recording, and facial/eye movement recording, can be housed on many types of computer and peripheral devices, including USB drives, video cameras, PCs, servers, and cloud-based repositories. It is important to keep track of every location where even a small amount of this data has been stored, especially if your data is sensitive or private. If several USB drives were used to transfer data to a central PC, were the files cleaned off of each drive? The same goes for data cards in video cameras. If files were transferred as attachments to e-mail messages, all related message files should be cleared from any temporary folders on both the sender and recipient devices. Does the PC have an automatic backup to an exterior drive or cloud-based storage? You'll need to make sure that you caught all the possible locations where your data may have migrated. Now, having warned you to keep track of all the places where your data may be stored, it's important to note that saving a backup is not a bad idea. Technology can fail or be hacked into at an alarming rate, and you put your content at risk if you don't keep duplicate files in an alternate data storage location.

Whether in paper or digital, be sure to keep your actual testing instrument(s) in a physical or digital folder. Hard work went into designing the questions used on your usability studies, and even if you do not reuse those exact questions, you may want to review them to extract the correct wording for a new study. Try to organize your material in a consistent way, so that someone else would be able to find it if you retire or leave the institution.

Five years are frequently given as a reasonable time period to retain collected data. Once you're ready to get rid of your data, there are a couple of things to consider. Destroying data collected on paper most often requires shredding at the very least, and may need to go so far as incineration. You'll need to check with your institution to see how strict they are about data disposal. In extreme cases, you may be advised to blacken out identifying information such as names, social security numbers, or library/university IDs with a dark permanent marker as an added precaution before the shedding takes place.

Destroying digital data completely can be tricky because of all the places that your data may live on in temp files or in the cloud, as mentioned earlier. Disposing digital data can be particularly difficult after five years' time because it may be hard to find all the places that the data has gone. The computers that were used for the study may have been replaced during the five-year window, institutional backup methods may have changed, and employee researchers may have moved on to other positions without tracking where they stored their data.

Study Follow Through

After your studies are done, you've presented your findings, and made your data storage decisions, your next big step is to do something with the results that you found. The next several chapters will provide you with ideas and practical steps for improving the discovery system experience for your patrons.

Chapter 3

Discovery System Configuration

Now that you have a good sense of how your discovery system is being used, or not being used, how do you begin to make changes to improve its usability? The most important thing to keep in mind is to trust your study results. A lot of work goes into planning, implementing, and compiling results for usability studies, and that will all be wasted time and effort if you do not follow through and try to fix the problems that you found. When analyzing usability results, fight the urge to allow your mind to wander back to the discussions that took place when your discovery system was initially set up, and instead, trust your data. There is nothing to be gained by rehashing the rationale that went into data decisions and web design. Forget the good intentions and focus on the usability reality.

Before you embark on a wholesale redesign of your system, recognize your limits. Be aware of what you can and cannot change. This may sound a bit like the Serenity Prayer (a common name for a prayer authored by the American theologian Reinhold Niebuhr), but it is good to understand the features of your discovery system that can be improved by changing the wording or by reorganizing the placement of content or limiters on the your web pages, and what functionality can't be changed because the structure of your discovery system prevents you from doing so. You can sometimes find technology work-arounds to solve problems that can't be adjusted within the discovery system environment itself, but if you take this route, be sure to let your vendor know that their system isn't meeting your needs. You may not be the only client who'd like to make changes in a specific area of your system. Vendors frequently issue software updates, and your request for change may provide the weight needed to push that technology request to the top of the company's to-do list.

It is likely that your usability study identified some glaringly obvious things to change in your discovery system. If you conducted a scavenger hunt-type usability study with multiple questions, chances are good that practically every user struggled with, or perhaps downright bombed, at least one question. These are the kinds of questions that can make a researcher tense up every time a new participant approaches that point in the study because you know that it's not going to end well. This kind of data, while slightly painful for the researcher, is actually useful because it will help you easily identify an area screaming for help, and you will feel better about your entire discovery system if you address this problem first.

Once you have identified the most glaringly obvious problems like broken links or missing content, take a close look at the more ambiguous study results. These usually fall into two categories:

1. Tasks that some, but not all, users found difficult
2. Questions that were largely not answered in the most efficient way possible or the way a librarian would answer them.

When reviewing these results, it's important to consider the following question: do the results indicate that your system is broken? The bottom line for these two categories is that at least some users were able to complete the assigned task and found the correct answer. Because some participants were able to succeed, it's possible that your settings are good enough, and the differing results were caused by variations in participant research skills and experience. Be cautious about deciding to make large sweeping changes to your entire discovery system, based on a small percentage of poor results. As librarians, we want our tools to work well for every patron every time they use them, and we often have a tendency to go overboard when trying to fix things, which can end up making things more difficult instead of more simple. If you do decide to make changes, it's important to go back and do at least a minimal usability study of the fixed area to make sure that your changes have helped solve the problem that you identified from your usability data. Instead of a full-blown scavenger hunt or focus group, identify a few new patrons and pose only the problem question to them. Be sure not to change the wording of the usability questions from the original study.

DATA DECISIONS

The vendor that you selected probably provided help with the setup of your system, but if your usability studies showed that you're not getting what you want out of your discovery system, it's possible that the vendor's default settings may not be working for your particular environment. Some of the vendors encourage you to activate as much content as possible for your patrons to search, whether or not you have licensed access to it. However, you are the best judge as to whether or not this is the best approach for your patrons, and if your usability studies show that they're struggling to find good content in your system, one of the first things to look at is how you set up your data.

Like most decisions about the discovery system, your data decisions will be dependent upon the size of your library, your library type (public? 4-year academic? corporate?), the needs of your patrons, and what you are hoping to achieve with the discovery system. Unfortunately, as you'll notice during your setup, not all of your content will be easily accessible, though this has improved as discovery systems have become more popular and standardized. Most of the system vendors make it possible to search your library catalog and the bulk of your databases, but it may not be possible to include all your databases if they do not have established agreements with the system vendor. If your library is small and has limited research needs, this might be good enough for you. However, if you work at a high-level research library, the lack of one or two specialized databases might be a big concern for you and your patrons, and your usability testing might have shown this to be the case.

THE CATALOG
Local Catalog Data

If you asked your study participants to find a book or a DVD in the library, were they able to do so? If not, perhaps you need to review the way that you set up your catalog data in your discovery system. In the best of all worlds, a discovery system would search the current content of your catalog, provide all of the renewal and hold options of a traditional catalog, and contain enough bibliographic record detail to enable the search algorithms to work correctly, but not so much that the patron feels overwhelmed when looking at an item on the display side.

It is important to note that live searching of any database, including the library catalog, can significantly slow down the discovery system's electronic processes, which dramatically increases the time needed for the search and display of results. Patrons are accustomed to retrieving almost instant results, depending on the speed and bandwidth on their devices, from search engines like Google and do not have much patience to wait for results to appear. Both EBSCO's EDS team and Proquest's Summon have gotten around the problem of slow searching of live catalogs by working with libraries to extract their catalog data and send it to EBSCO on a predetermined schedule, which could be weekly or every few days depending on the size of the library's catalog holdings. For example, Penn State University sends a daily file to Proquest via FTP, which contains catalog additions, deletions, and updates. This canned data speed up the search process for the patron because the search does not need to go outside the EBSCO server configuration and can be managed with all the other EBSCO-hosted data. However, what the patron gains in speed, they lose in data accuracy. Searching canned data means that new items added to the catalog between updates won't show up in a discovery system search until the next data load, which is not ideal. This also means that items that have been withdrawn between updates won't be removed from the discovery system until the next data load. Most librarians would prefer to have their searches to show exactly what they own in real time, especially if they have a high volume of acquisitions and time-sensitive content. When you set up your system, you need to decide the level of catalog data discrepancy that you can comfortably tolerate, but it may be time to review that decision. On the bright side, even though the bibliographic records are static in the EDS and are only updated weekly, they do show real-time availability information by connecting to your local catalog through z39.50 protocol.

If your discovery system catalog content is tied to your OCLC holdings, like the Worldcat Discovery system, and you found that you were missing content during your usability study, it could be because your holdings aren't up to date in Worldcat, which can be a daunting problem to fix. For anyone unfamiliar with what this means, OCLC has made a business of not only providing high-quality MARC records to libraries to be reused in their local catalogs, but they also ask their member libraries to keep track of their own holdings on the OCLC platform, so that other libraries or patrons can see which library owns what item, and then order that item via interlibrary loan (ILL). Traditionally, for an OCLC member library, adding a new item to their collection has meant cataloging it both locally in their library management system and also marking it as owned by that library on the OCLC record. If your staff has not been meticulous about adding and deleting holdings in OCLC as local collections ebb and flow, the OCLC holdings can become out of step with actual holdings, which means that OCLC-based catalog data in your discovery system will not be accurate. Staff changes such as retirement and shifting cataloging responsibilities, can lead to gaps in training that can wreak havoc on the maintenance of OCLC holdings.

Another problem with basing your discovery system catalog content on OCLC holdings is that not all your materials may be cataloged in OCLC. If you own archival records unique to your library, it might be up to your catalogers to create a record for those items in OCLC, which can be a painstaking process if you want to be sure to catalog it correctly according to Bibliographic Standards. Records for archives material may have been added to the local catalog with a quick entry rather than taking the time to add a new record in OCLC, and libraries in this situation would not want to lose that access when going to the OCLC-based catalog in their discovery system.

In the past, some library staff saw OCLC primarily as a place to mark materials that they'd be willing to loan to other libraries via ILL. If they owned a collection that they were never planning to loan, like archival material or LPs, they may not have added this content to OCLC, and it would take a great deal of work and energy to add that material in order to make it visible in a discovery system. For example, the Genesee Community College library, where one of the authors works, owns a large music LP collection that was never cataloged in OCLC because it was not intended to be loaned to other libraries. If the librarians had decided to add this collection, they could have tried to take advantage of OCLC's ILL deflection protocols to prevent unwanted ILL lending requests, but the protocols are based on material type, such as sound recordings, and can't be narrowed to a particular collection like CDs (which are loanable) vs. LPs (which are not). Other types of collections that libraries might not have added to OCLC could be a rotating McNaughton Adult Lease collection from Brodart, where the titles change frequently and are not permanently owned by the library, or materials in a Reserves collection that might be owned by faculty and change based on the courses being taught during a semester. These are just some of the reasons why your OCLC data may not be completely accurate, which will affect your discovery system data if your local holdings records are tied to OCLC.

External Catalog Data

Along with making decisions about your own catalog data, you may also have had the option to add access to other libraries' catalogs in your discovery system. Are you part of a consortium that has a union catalog? Do you partner with local libraries and have an interest in adding their catalog holdings to your discovery system? Did you want to allow your patrons to search the entire Worldcat system? The way that you answered these questions will depend on the savviness of your patrons and on their ability to parse and organize large amounts of data. Did your usability testing show that your users are overwhelmed with too many results? If so, you may need to go back and decrease the number of catalogs that you included in your discovery system. Remember, the more content you add to your system, the more results your users will see. This seems obvious, but it can make a big difference in how easy your system is to use and navigate.

Local Catalog Tools

One thing to note about catalog data usability in your discovery system is that if your patrons use the discovery system to locate physical materials instead of using the traditional catalog, they will lose access to local catalog tools. These tools vary by vendor, but most native catalogs provides the patron with the option to sign in to view their loans, see if they have any fines, renew items, or place items on hold. If your vendor imports your catalog data and hosts it on their platform, your patrons will lose the local catalog framework and tools. You can get around the missing "hold" option by setting up an ILL link and letting your patrons request items that you own, but it's up to you whether or not you want to allow patrons to request items that are currently on the shelf. The discovery vendor can help you design a link that will display all the time or it can work with your z39.50 protocol, to only display when the item is checked out or in a non-loan category. However, this is a clumsy work-around. Vendors are aware of this problem, and are making strides to try to incorporate local catalog functionality into their discovery systems. EBSCO staff reported—at the recent SUNY Librarians Association conference in Binghamton, New York—that they're working on tighter ILS integration and that it's now possible to place a hold in EDS for items from the Worldshare Management System (Collier, 2016).

DATABASES

The more databases that you add to your discovery system, the more results the patrons will get when they perform a search, and this can affect the usability of your system. Most of the discovery system vendors will offer you the option to search all their indexed content, even if you do not subscribe to the source database. This can give your patrons a more complete picture of all the resources available on their topic, but your usability study may have shown you that your patrons can become confused if they're not able to get to the full text of the content that displays in your result lists or if they're overwhelmed by the huge numbers of results for their searches. If your library is a "more is better' kind of place, where your patrons have strong critical thinking skills and possess expert searching skills, opening up your system to all available data might work for you. However, if your library patrons are less sophisticated researchers and have more limited scholarly needs, you might want to review your database selection settings and only activate the databases to which you subscribe, so that the majority of the search results will give the patron access to full-text content. Your usability testing can help you determine the right balance of results to research needs, by looking at how your patrons interact with the discovery system. The testing will help you find the line between what's enough data and what might cause too much confusion and frustration.

During the setup of your discovery system, you may have found that some of your databases weren't included on the list of possible databases that you could activate in your system. This problem is diminishing as publishers grow more comfortable working with discovery system vendors, but there may be contractual issues, such as vendors like Proquest being reluctant to give their data to competing discovery vendors like EBSCO. If the database that you wanted wasn't available in your vendor's content, they may offer you other ways to access your database, such as a widget where patrons can redo their searches, or a separate link, or other ways to access this specialized content. It's up to you to decide if your patrons are smart enough to handle this option or if it's better to leave that database out of the discovery mix. Usability testing on the group of patrons who are most likely to use this content is a good way to tell if the alterative access is worth keeping.

Recommended Database Option in Summon

If you are concerned that some of your specialized databases will get lost in the discovery system shuffle, there are ways to highlight stand-alone databases within the discovery system environment. Summon allows libraries to set up direct links to recommended databases, which when implemented appear as special text or in a special place on the results page, in order to alert the user that these results are separate from the "normal" results. The recommendation display can be designed to include the database title, a brief description, and a link directly to the database. In the Summon admin area, you can create a list of keyword triggers that will automatically display appropriate database recommendations. For example, if you work in a college library and you know that one of your professors uses the same research assignment every semester, you could use keywords from that assignment to trigger reminders that there are specialized databases that can be used for additional research.

Keyword triggers can be a handy way to provide access to your stand-alone databases. In the college setting, students are sometimes told by their professors to use specific databases like Medline or JSTOR. If you check your search analytics, you may be surprised to see listings for searches for CINAHL or other databases that your patrons have been told to use. You can set up keyword triggers to display a link to any database name typed into your discovery system. Depending on the overall speed of your discovery system, it may be faster for your users to type even part of the database title in the search box, and then click on the recommended database link than it is to search for the database name through other channels from the library web page.

Your decision whether or not to implement the recommended database feature should be based on the demographics of your user population. Advanced researchers will appreciate the offer of a specialized resource where they can focus on their subject area, rather than having to weed through the general discovery system results from nonacademic sources or from databases outside their field. However, for inexperienced researchers, the recommended databases can be a double-edged sword. It can be helpful for new users if they were instructed to search in a particular database, as a user told to search in JSTOR may naively type JSTOR in the discovery system search, and if recommended databases keyword triggers have been implemented, the user will accidentally discover the direct link to the database. On the other hand, with the recommended links so prominently displayed at the top of the results screen, it can be easy for a novice user to click on one and lose themselves in an entirely new system with a brand new search form that does not remember the search that they just did in the discovery system. If the new database opens in a new window, they may have difficulty finding their way back to their initial search.

Database Selection and Branding

An interesting side note to consider when selecting your discovery system databases is how you'll market your system. If you're unable to activate all your library's content, can you still market it as "one-stop shopping" for the library? What's the smallest number of databases that you can leave out and still claim that it's searching "everything"? These are the kinds of questions that can drive nitpicky librarians crazy, but probably have no effect on the average user, who won't notice if an obscure, rarely used database is missing from the discovery system search. Also, there's usually enough overlap in database coverage so that the loss of one database may be covered by the citation holdings of another source. Your system vendor can run a coverage comparison or resource analysis report for you to help you check for overlaps and gaps in your local collections content.

EBOOK COLLECTIONS

If you tested your patrons' ability to find eBooks in your discovery system, you may have found that the discovery process does not always go smoothly. If your library purchased an entire eBook collection, it should work fine in your discovery system because access is set up by a toggle on/off switch for each database or catalog. However, things can get more complicated if you've only purchased individual titles and not the whole collection. Summon will let you activate individual title in a collection, but in the EBSCO's EDS, it's all or nothing where eBooks are concerned. In EDS, there is no way to pick out and activate individual titles from databases like Gale Cengage's Gale Virtual Reference Library or Salem Press. If you choose to activate the whole collection, it means that your patrons will get search results for titles that are part of this collection but to which you don't have access, which can be frustrating. eBooks are notoriously difficult to get via ILL because of licensing problems, and activating all the eBooks in a collection will only make your patrons want what they can't have. One way to work around this problem is to choose to not activate the eBook package and to rely solely on the eBook's MARC from your OPAC. Note that this option will only work if the practice at your library is to add eBook records to your OPAC. OPAC eBook items will come up in your search results as catalog records, although the MARC record may have more limited keywords, table of contents, and description information than the record in the eBook collection, which makes it less searchable. It would be great if one day you could pick the individual titles from the collection rather than picking wholesale. Are you listening, EBSCO? Be aware that some databases, such as JSTOR or Credo, where you might only purchase part of their offerings, have the same problem in EDS, where switching them on makes all their content available, not just the content to which you subscribe. More dead-end results with no full text except via ILL mean more frustration for your patrons.

One thing that can make it challenging for your patrons to find eBooks in your collection is the way that your vendor sets up limits and filters. A peculiarity with Summon is that it has only one category for limiting books which is "Book/

eBook" and that cannot be separated into print book or eBook, regardless of how these materials are cataloged in your OPAC. There are many reasons why a user may have a need for a print book format instead of eBook or vice versa:

- Their home Internet access may be spotty, so they may prefer print over eBooks
- Many studies have shown that college students still prefer to read print rather than eBooks (Derla, 2016)
- On the eBook side, a patron may want to be able to programmatically search the electronic version of the book for their keywords
- The patron might want the flexibility of being able to use an eBook even if someone else has it checked out, a multiuser model that isn't available for print materials

Finding eBooks in a Summon search can be a challenge, even when limiting the results to books/eBooks. If your library acquisitions policy has changed to mandate eBook purchase over print copies, sorting by date can sometimes cause the eBooks to float to the top of the list, but this is not a given. A relevancy search can also bring the most current additions, which may be eBooks, to the top of the results list. Because many libraries are switching to eBook purchases over print because of cost, storage, and usability concerns, a patron who uses a discovery system to just browse the physical (not virtual) stacks may have to scan through pages of results before finding print books that they can find on their local library shelves. The inability to distinguish between print and online offerings may be a valid reason for continuing your catalog as a separate entity and retaining a prominent link to the catalog from your library website.

SETTING UP YOUR USER INTERFACE

Search Decisions

Your usability testing will quickly indicate how your participants interacted with your discovery system search box. If you decided to default to basic search rather than the advanced search as a starting point, did that seem to work for your participants? Most patrons are familiar with the basic Google-like search box, and you may have found that your participants understood how to use that box. However, if you work at a more specialized location, did you find that your participants tried to fine-tune their search during the search preparation, rather than using limits and filtering after seeing their search results? If so, you might be better off choosing to offer the advanced search, with all of its presearch filters, as the default search for your patrons. If you work with a mix of patrons, some of whom are power users and some of whom aren't, you might want to default to the basic search, but design your access to the discovery system so that the option to switch to advanced search is readily apparent.

Results List
Display

What did your usability testing show you about your participants' response to your discovery system results page(s)? Did it seem to make sense to them? Could they identify the list of results? Was it too busy and overwhelming? You can use your participant responses to help you refine and revise your results page to make it more useful for your patrons. Most of the vendors let you change the number of columns that you display in the results page, they let you control how much information you display for each result entry (title, source, abstract, etc.), and they let you control the placement of things like filters, widgets, images, social media links, and other content. You may be tempted to go overboard and provide your patrons with any and all options offered by your vendor, but try to take a step back and look at the results page from the perspective of one of the personas that you developed back in your study planning phase. What's too much information? What do you really need to meet your research goals?

EBSCO's EDS lets you decide how many columns you want to display on the results list, ranging from one to three. If you choose three columns, you can still default to display only two, but the third column can be accessed by clicking on a small pop-out panel graphic. Think carefully before you decide to go with the hidden panel option. How many of your patrons will notice the pop-out arrow? Is it worth it to put anything important in this column? Some libraries choose to use this hidden column for access to specialized databases, or for widgets like a list of LibGuides that might be related to the search term. Bear in mind that the only way that your patrons might learn about this hidden column is from a library instruction class, or if one of their professors or peers tells them about it.

In EDS, you can decide if you want your limits to appear in the left side column or the right side column, or if you want any limits to show up at all. Our recommendation would be to put your limits in the left side column because that's the standard for common websites like Target or Home Depot, but you can use usability testing to see what works best for your patrons. The thing to keep in mind is that asking your patrons what they want is never a wasted exercise. We want our tools to work as well as they can for our users, and we're sometimes blinded by our years of library experience and knowledge. Real user feedback is golden when you're working on your discovery system design.

Another thing to consider when you're looking at your results list is how many results do you want to show on one page? Remember that most patrons are reluctant to page through multiple pages of results and are hoping that the content they need is listed in the first few results on the page. You may have seen this behavior during your usability testing. We'd all love our patrons to be diligent researchers who keep looking through their results until they find the best material, but that's often an unrealistic expectation. With that in mind, you might want to decide to display more than 20 or 30 results on a page rather than 10 or another small amount. Your patron's attention span is fleeting, and you want to keep them on that first results page as long as possible because they're not always likely to keep paging through results. On the other hand, if you decide to set your system to default to 50 or more results to a page, that might be too overwhelming for your users. The best way to fine-tune these setting options is by talking to your patrons and asking them what number of results would work best for them.

Something else to consider is how detailed you want to make your result item display on the results list. For most libraries, a succinct entry is better than a lengthy one because you're trying to keep your patron's attention and keep them scrolling down the page. You don't want to give them too much information upfront. It's useful to show the title of the item, the author, the source, its library location, and availability if it's a physical item, and if it's an electronic item you'll want the patron to know right away whether or not it's available in full text. While this shortened display is good for most libraries, your patrons may have different needs. You may need to display the original database source for your results because a faculty member on your campus will only let his students use articles that originally came from JSTOR. If you work in a public library, it might be very important to provide patron reviews for items on the results list. Will material type icons help your patrons identify what's a physical item and what's an electronic result? Each library is different, and usability testing can help you design your results list to best meet the needs of your patrons.

One thing that's handy about a discovery system like EDS is that no matter how you design your results list to display as a default, you can also let your patron change the display to meet their own needs by using the "page options" dropdown. The EDS page options lets the user decide how much information they want to see for item in the results list (title only, detailed record, brief, or standard); how many results they'd like to see per page, ranging from 5 to 50; and how many columns they'd like to see on the page.

Relevancy Ranking and Sorting

A couple of other things to consider when designing your discovery system results list are relevancy ranking and sorting options. You may have no control over the relevancy ranking that your vendor uses to pull results from their data repository. However, it's important to understand the methods that they're using, and make sure that these methods best fit the needs of your patrons. Are you getting the kinds of search results that you hope to see? If not, it can be worth it to contact your vendor to talk about how you can improve your relevancy ranking.

Most vendors will give you the option to change your default sorting method for your results list. For most libraries, it makes the most sense to sort results by relevance in order to better match your patron's search. But, if your patrons are power users who can craft a good search, and they're most concerned about the currency of the results, you might want to set up your results list to sort by "Date Newest." Again, usability testing is an excellent way to figure out what's most important to your patrons when they're looking for information in your discovery system.

Facets and Filters

One of the best things about discovery systems are their varied lists of facets and filters, which are familiar to anyone who's ever searched the Amazon.com website or most other web shopping sites. People like filters. Filters make it easy to fine-tune your search and find what you need. So, filters are good, but are the filters that you picked working for your patrons? Do they understand the terminology? Do you have the ability to change this wording? How do you decide which filters to display?

Filters fall into several different categories: location, whether or not the item has full text, the level of complexity of the item (scholarly, peer reviewed, etc.), date of publication, source type, language, content provider, and more. Results page real estate is limited, and it's up to you to decide which limits are most important to your patrons. This is something that you can test with a card sorting exercise, where you ask your patrons to identify their preferred limits and the order of limits that makes the most sense to them. Is full-text access the most important thing for your patron? Then, this should be the first option on your list of filters. Do your faculty insist that their students use scholarly journals for research papers? Then, this filter also needs to be prominent.

Speaking of scholarly journals, it's time to talk about a common problem that pops up frequently when reviewing the results of usability tests: library terminology. The words that we use when speaking to students, or when designing research tools like discovery system interfaces, are not always as comprehensible to students as we assume them to be. Terms that are second nature to us like "abstract" or "pdf" are not always familiar to our patrons. EBSCO's User Research Group conducted a study on this terminology problem in early 2015 and found that "Library-ese is one of the most reported issues identified in user testing. Unfamiliar terms are barriers to users fully utilizing library resources/services" ("Do Your Students," 2015). Bear this in mind when you're setting up your system and picking limiters to display. Your vendor may allow you to choose your own wording for your filters or limiters, which can give you the flexibility to make your system reflect common usage for your particular location. For example, if you know that your faculty use the term "peer-reviewed" journal instead of "scholarly" journal, you can change the limit display in your discovery system to match the wording that your students hear in their classes.

One filter that can be tricky to use in the EBSCO's EDS is "Available in Library Collection." This filter is directly related to the decisions you made about what content to include in your discovery system. If you decided to add all the content provided by the vendor, whether or not you subscribe to that content, this filter can be used to narrow your search results to only that content that's actually accessible to the patron. This may make sense to a librarian, but consider this limit from the patron's perspective: they're searching for resources using a library tool; isn't everything that comes up part of the library collection? You'll need to think hard about whether or not you want to activate everything and use this limit to narrow results, or if you want to, limit what you activate to only your licensed content and hide this filter option.

There are a few more filters to consider when reviewing your discovery system settings. Do your faculty require their students to use articles from specific databases like JSTOR or CINAHL for assignments? If so, you'll want to highlight the "original source" filter so that your students can identify content that came from one of those sources. Do you want to provide your patrons with the ability to narrow their searches by discipline? If so, you'll want to make sure that that limit is displayed in a prominent location. Designing an effective search environment can be a delicate balance of offering enough limits and filters, but not so many that the options become overwhelming to your patrons.

It's a good idea to contact your vendor if your usability testing found that you were missing an important filter or that your participants misunderstood how the filters worked. Your vendor might be willing to create a special limiter for you. For example, EBSCO recently created a "print book" limiter for a campus in the SUNY system because the library staff noticed that their students wanted to be able to differentiate between print and electronic book results in their discovery system (Collier, 2016). If you can think of a way to identify a set of data, based on MARC fields in the bibliographic record or on other database fields, then your vendor can probably create a custom filter for you.

Additional Tools

Discovery system vendors are constantly working on new features to add to their systems, and it's up to you to decide which tools will be useful for your patrons and which ones will just lead to more confusion. You can create short, targeted usability studies to address the necessity of individual tools, or you could test several at one time. Whether or not you decide to implement any of these extra features will depend upon the savviness of your patrons.

We can't cover all the available tools in this book because there are too many, and more are being created even as we write, but here are a few of the more common types:

Bibliographic Tools: These give your patrons the ability to save searches and records from their results lists. They usually require the patron to set up a separate account with the vendor so that they can save their content within the platform. Some vendors are working to set up connections with outside Cloud platforms like Google Drive, so that patrons can save their content to their personal storage locations without needing a vendor sign-on.

Citation Tools: Most vendors give you the option to activate citation tools for the big three citation styles: APA, MLA, and Chicago. These tools can be a useful starting point for students who need to create citations for papers, but like any auto-generated citation, they're not 100 percent accurate all the time, and students will still need to know the rules of citation and double-check the results.

Social Media Tools: Most vendors will let you decide whether or not you want your patrons to be able to share searches or their results to social media platforms like Twitter, Facebook, and more. It's up to you whether or not you think that this would be useful or whether it just adds clutter to your screen. In a similar vein, vendors now offer the option to incorporate Goodreads or Google Books results and other outside media.

Research Starters: EBSCO lets you activate their canned Research Starters, which is designed to appear at the top of your results list if the search matches one of the predefined summary areas. For example, a search for trees in EDS gives you a Research Starter for "Stems (Botany)" from the Salem Press *Encyclopedia of Science*. It can be a helpful starting point for patrons who might need some extra help with their topic.

Automated Query Expansion: This Summon feature expands upon and corrects the search terms entered by the patron in the discovery system search box. It corrects commonly misspelled words and adds synonyms or other common terms for the searched item if they have been preprogrammed for the terms. While this is an automatic addition, there is a linked option for the user to only search the terms that they originally entered.

Placards: EBSCO lets you create your own top of the results list entry for commonly searched terms like "library hours," or the name of a particular database like JSTOR, or a commonly used journal at your location. You can create permanent placards or you can set them up to only display for a particular time period, perhaps when you're hosting an event and you suspect that people might search the discovery system for information about that event. You can design the placard to appear in response to variations on your term such as "MLA," "MLA citation," "citation help," and so forth. The box itself can look however you want it to appear, and can be a simple link to your citation information pages or a lengthy review of the styles, whatever you prefer.

Best Bet Recommendations: Similar to placards in EBSCO's EDS, Summon lets you prepopulate your system with answers to patron questions that will not be found in your databases. For patrons used to searching in Google, it seems like a discovery system search box should search all things library related, not just your catalog and databases. For example, questions such as "What are the library hours?," "Do you have photocopiers?," or "How do I cite a DVD in MLA style?" If you check your most requested search terms in your system analytics, you will be amazed at the number of times these questions are asked by your patrons, and yes, they are often asked in the whole language format. If you don't prepopulate your discovery system to answer these types of questions, most of these queries are met with an error message or a "your search resulted in 0 results" message, which is confusing to your patrons and may make them think that the system is either broken, or stupid, or both. It would be great if you could add a Google site search for your library web pages to your discovery system, but until that technology evolves, your best bet is to add answers to frequently asked questions like hours, library floor maps, links to style guide help websites, electronic course reserves, and help guides for specific, perennial assignments. It is worth the time and effort to establish these best bet choices in order to improve your user satisfaction with your discovery system.

Spotlighting: This Summon feature lets you set your discovery system to highlight news articles and images in your results list. The news results display with a *News results for "search term"* heading, and they present the most current news about the search term. The slight offsetting of these entries, though subtle, does draw the user's eye to the section. The images feature presents the patron with a group of thumbnail images if there are any images in the collection that match the patron's search. The thumbnails are displayed in a row, similar to the way they appear in many Internet search engines. Clicking on the thumbnail leads users to the content page on which the image appeared. Images can be from local, special collections, commercial databases, or open-source repositories.

Topic Explorer: This Summon feature offers users additional help in defining their search terms, finding self-help options, and even offers personal attention from a librarian. The Topic Explorer options appear on the results list after a search has been completed, in individual, window-type boxes on the right-hand side of the screen. They are clearly delineated so as not to be confused with the original result citations, and they will only appear if the patron's search terms match terms and criteria predefined by the library. There are several Topic Explorer options:

   Definition: The search term is matched to a definition on either a commercial reference source, such as Gale Virtual Reference Library, Credo Reference, or a website such as Wikipedia. Libraries are at liberty to activate any or all of these sources.

   Suggested Librarian: The search term is matched with a librarian who has experience with the searched topic and the patron is provided with that librarian's profile, which can contain the librarian's name, e-mail, and even a photo if desired.

   Related Topics: Summon uses the history of previous searches to find related topics that might help the patron find what they need. Clicking on one of the topic links automatically places that text in the search box with quotations around it and starts the search process.

   Recommended Research Guides: This option lets you provide links to your homegrown research guides, such as Springshare's LibGuides product, based on the user's search topic.

As mentioned previously, vendors have teams constantly developing new features for their discovery systems. Here are few new developments (Collier, 2016) that may be in common use by the time this book is published:

StackMaps Integration: If you use StackMaps with your traditional OPAC to help patrons pinpoint the exact physical location of an item in your building, EBSCO can integrate this service into EDS.

Contextual Help: St. Louis Community College is piloting a pop-up suggestion box, similar to pop-up chat, which will appear depending on search results. If the results list is book heavy, it will remind the patron that academic journals are also available. If the patron did not limit to full text, it will suggest that as a possible limiter.

Autocorrected Search: Borrowing from the Google model, EBSCO's EDS can auto-correct searches with obvious typos.

Apps: EBSCO's discovery service engineers and user research teams are working on a "Chipotle app" that will let patrons swipe through results and select the ones that interest them.

Getting to Full Text

Just like on the results list, you have control over what you choose to display in your full record view. Do you want your patrons to see all the bibliographic information for a result, or just the most relevant parts like title, author, source, and year of publication? Do you need to display the original database source for the material? Do you want to automatically display the abstract, or do you think that your patrons will confuse the abstract with the full text? How prominent and findable are your full-text links? Do your patrons understand the terminology that you're using (e.g., html, pdf, etc.)? Usability testing can help you answer these kinds of questions.

Interlibrary Loan and Link Resolvers

A huge results list is useless to patrons if they can't get to the content for the best results. If your patrons are adept at using ILL to request items from your databases, then you might want to activate as much content as is available in your discovery system and let the patrons use the ILL link to request items that are not available in full text. If, however, your patrons are less sophisticated and are easily confused, you might want to limit the number of databases that you activate and try to provide only material that will be full text and easily accessible.

One of the important things to check during your usability study is whether or not your students are able to use your link resolvers to get to the full text of a search result, or to order that full text via ILL if it's not available. Some individual factors to test are user recognition of an abstract vs. full-text content, familiarity with html and pdf full-text formats, relatability to the terms ILL, and the ability to transpose parts of a citation into ILL form fields if automatic form completion is not an option.

You can work with the discovery system vendor to decide how you want to use your link resolver: do you want it to show for everything? For only items that aren't full text? Do you want to show the ILL link right away? Do you want to include purchase on demand options? These are all things to consider adding or changing if you find that your patrons aren't finding the content that they need. Some discovery systems like EDS offer smartlinks to full text, but it can be complicated to get these links to work with your off-site proxy server; so, you might want to rely on your link resolver to do the work of getting content to the patron.

Summon has put a great deal of effort into improving the user experience with its link resolver technology and linking interface. Librarian anecdotes and published usability studies (Imler and Eichelberger, 2011) have proven that nonlibrarian users struggle to follow through on obtaining the full text of articles when the article is more than one click away, when an error message is received, or when users are required to redo a search through an individual database search page. Users who experience these issues will often attempt to back their way out of the search by using browser buttons, or will just abandon the search altogether. To combat these user problems, Summon took a two-pronged approach to improve their 360 Link link resolver. The company sought to increase the reliability of linked materials and also to improve the user interface if linkage was not possible. The traditional OpenURL method of link resolving has had a low success rate, mostly due to incomplete or incompatible metadata (Price and Trainor, 2010). To improve user satisfaction, Summon encouraged the development of Index-Enhanced Direct Linking (IEDL) technology. IEDL delivers successful links nearly 100 percent of the time, by combining metadata with the full-text content obtained from database providers. One noticeable difference with IEDL use is that it is able to connect more directly to an article or book chapter, which combats the need to recreate a search in the original database interface, as happens with OpenURL linking technology. For content providers who will not allow access to their full text offerings, Summon continues to use OpenURL in addition to IEDL.

In addition to the implementation of IEDL in order to improve content matching, Summon engineers and web designers also improved the linkage interface that pops up when a full text link resolver search fails or when an item is unavailable in full text. A common complaint of previous linking formats was that the design of the link resolver screens often looked like commercial websites rather than academic web pages, and they were easily ignored by users because they resembled advertising banners on other websites. The new format appears as a sidebar frame on the right-hand side of the screen, and it's become a seamless part of the Summon system rather than a separate pop-up navigation window. The 360 sidebar is highly customizable and can be personalized to include your library or university branding. The sidebar also includes optional panels that can offer the user the option to choose their article from another database if multiple databases are available, a clear link to ILL forms and even links to librarian information or live reference chats (ProQuest).

Access

Another thing to consider when reviewing your discovery system options is the point at which you want to make your patrons login for off-site access to licensed content. Most databases require the user to login if they are outside the library's Internet network, because their full-text access licenses only apply to verified members of the library's community (i.e., students, faculty, staff, or community members). Some libraries prefer to force the proxy login before the patron begins to search the discovery system so that the patron won't need to login to get to the full text of an article, while other libraries might choose to provide guest access to the search, but force a login if the user wants to see the full text. One way that you could test which scenario works best for your community would be to do A/B testing on the two options.

Here are some things to consider when deciding if you need to change the way that you allow access to your discovery system:

- The system will contain a mix of licensed full-text data and nonlicensed material such as library catalog records.
- Your patrons may be used to having open access to your holdings because most library catalogs are designed to allow users to search without logging in.
- Open access can be handy for community members who are not licensed to use database content with the library, but who may want to know if the library owns an item in which they're interested.
- Open access is also useful for other librarians, who might be curious to see how an item was cataloged or who are trying to make regional collection development decisions.

WEBSITE ACCESS TO THE DISCOVERY SYSTEM

The way that your discovery system is made visible to your patrons is fundamental to its success. There are many things that can hinder successful web design and implementation of your system on your library's website:

- A team of implementers that don't agree on the look, language, and placement of the system.
- Page ownership: Many libraries do not control their own pages, and their staff has to work with other members of the college community or governing bodies to make changes to the content.
- Colleagues who are resistant to change the way that they do business at the reference desk or in the classroom, who don't want to see the new service on the library's homepage.

It does no good to spend months setting up the content for a discovery system only to have access to that system buried in subpages on your website. This can be a touchy political situation, especially if you don't have buy-in from all members of your staff. If your staff doesn't see the need to offer a simple search box on your homepage for the system, it can sabotage the success of the system. Performing usability studies can give you the data that you need to persuade your campus constituents that web design improvements are necessary.

Benchmarking against Other Libraries

The odds are very good that your library is not the first to implement the discovery system you just purchased. If your usability studies highlighted problems with your web design, it can be helpful to review other library interfaces to see how they implemented their instance of your selected discovery system. Your vendor will probably gladly share a list of their top library customers. Usually, links to discovery systems are easily located on a library's main web page and are seldom password protected, giving the researcher easy access.

Benchmarking can be done by one individual or a small team. Select three or four discovery interfaces from other libraries and rate them on several areas:

- Discoverability
- Overall look and feel
- Navigation
- Ease of task completion

You will want to outline your benchmarking points and make sure that all members of your team judge each site using the same criteria. Be sure to note any aspects of each site you liked or disliked and why. If you notice that sites you are benchmarking are cookie cutter images of each other, this may mean that the discovery system is quite rigid and doesn't leave much room for creativity or flexibility of design or navigation. One downfall of benchmarking is that researchers can be lulled into thinking that a certain style is "good design" because several sites have used it. Keep in mind what your parents always said about you following after your friends if they all jumped off a cliff. Benchmarking can be particularly helpful to determine the overall look and feel of your site, to decide if and where to include add-in features and for finding alternatives to library jargon.

Search Box Design

During your usability study, were your patrons able to find your search box and were they able to use it efficiently? If not, here are some things to consider when revising your search box design.

If you're trying to mirror the patron's experience with Google and other Internet search sites, the best way to do that is by designing a clean, simple search box, with obvious tools and options. Unlike the design of the discovery system results pages, the discovery system vendors will give you free range in designing your box, and you will have many options to consider:

- What kind of searches will you offer in the initial box? Keyword only? Title? Author? Subject? And how will you display these options? In a drop-down, radio button, tabs?
- Will you offer the patron the option of switching to an advanced search right from the search box, or leave it simple?
- Will you include information about what the search is covering, that is, a tagline to tell the patron that they'll be searching the catalog and the databases at the same time?

Your answers to these questions will vary greatly, depending on the aesthetics of your web pages, the makeup of your audience, and the needs of your library staff members.

If after presenting your usability study results, you're still having trouble getting discovery system buy-in from colleagues who don't want to lose the functionality of your local catalog or a database-only search, you can consider creating a tabbed search box on your website. This lets the patron (or the library staff member) change the type of search they're doing, depending on their need. The tabbed box takes up less real estate than creating a separate search box for each search type, and it's a commonly used, familiar interface.

If your usability studies showed you that your system isn't being used as well as you'd like it to be used, you may need to redesign your library homepage. This is a major undertaking for any library, particularly if the web page maintenance is managed from outside the library. Web design and management is especially difficult if you don't have skilled web design staff on your team. The discovery system vendors can help you design a simple search box, but if you need it to have specific campus colors or logos, you'll need to do the design work on your own. The best thing to do when considering revising your discovery system search box is to go online and look at how other libraries have implemented these types of boxes. It's a lot easier to come up with your own design when you've spent some time learning about how other places have done it. Also, it is easier to present your team with design options when you have visuals to show them, rather than describing the box placement verbally.

Where you put the box on the page can directly impact how it's used. If the patron doesn't notice it, it will not be used. Visibility can be hampered by small font, poor color choices, and other bad design elements. At this point in the redesign process, you can use results from your usability focus groups or other testing, to determine which design and placement options are most noticeable and gain the most attention on the page.

It almost goes without saying that as you're designing your search box and placing it on your library web pages, remember to test it on multiple platforms: phone, tablet, laptop, and PC. The best practice in web design is to create a responsive page that resizes and works on any size screen. You can recruit your colleagues or other willing parties to help you test your design on their personal devices, to make sure that it will work in the way that you want it to work. Another thing to do that should go without saying, but is often forgotten, is to make sure that your site is accessible for screen readers and other assistive devices. Your vendors should be handling accessibility inside their product, but it's up to you to make sure that your search box design and other library web page features are accessible for all your patrons and their adaptive technology. There are plenty of websites that can help you learn more about accessibility testing for your site. A good site for accessibility testing is at WebAim.org. It offers the free WAVE web accessibility evaluation tool, provides reports and suggestions for improvement, is recognized, and can provide certification that your site is accessible.

Widgets

One of the best things about redesigning a discovery system search box for your library web pages is that you can then take that code and turn it into a widget or a self-contained chunk of code, which can then be deployed in other locations both on the library's web pages and on pages hosted by outside entities. If you happen to be an academic librarian, this code can be given to faculty or to your learning management system administrator, and it can be added to pages in learning management systems like Blackboard, Moodle, or others, so that students can search right from their course pages. The code can also be embedded in systems like LibGuides, which is a tool to manage library resources for specific courses, replacing the old print handouts of the past. The widget can be a valuable tool in providing access to the discovery system.

WEB IMPLEMENTATION

Beta Testing

Beta Testing has become standard practice when implementing new library systems or system improvements. Testing ahead of time helps to work out the kinks in data transfer and helps to verify if the system components that the discovery system company swears will work together really will.

It has become common to set up a "sandbox" or test server environment when testing a large system before purchase, or at least before full implementation takes place. This exploration site allows developers to experiment with code and loading of records in a safe environment that mirrors the reality of the real system. It is this type of sandbox environment that can allow for a small percentage of records to be added to test not only the back-end procedures, but also give some idea of searchability and user interface interaction. Due to the proprietary nature of discovery systems, the company may not provide a sandbox environment for experimentation. In that case, the library may have to rely on sales demonstrations and recommendations from current libraries using the system to determine if a purchase will take place. Once the system has been purchased, it is possible to do a limited records load and offer a "soft rollout" to a limited and select group of library staff and users that, in fact, mirrors a beta test.

One of the key factors to determine is who will have access to the beta test site. It will be easy to identify the data management and systems staff who will need access for technological reasons, but don't forget your front-end staff who will be promoting your system to your patrons. A beta test is the opportune time to gauge user reaction to the site's look and feel, and to work out any navigation issues. Problems worked out and corrected before the site goes public can save a lot of negative word of mouth, once the site goes live.

Introducing the beta site to a focus group is a good, controlled way to get user feedback without unleashing the site to the general public. In the focus group setting, the beta server URLs can be effectively hidden in order to control access to the site until you're ready for a real launch, and you can guide users to conduct predetermined searches and answer direct questions rather than letting them loose on the site.

Some libraries prefer to do a full, public release of the beta version. This method has both pros and cons (Table 3.1).

If you release the beta version to the general public, you will need a variety of reminders that it is only a test site. When marking the link, do not rely on the word "beta." Many people outside the IT world do not know what that means. "Test site" is a much better term, and "temporary test site" is even better. If your beta site was designed by your vendor to only contain a subset of your data, make sure to add prominent reminders on the site web pages to let people know that the search contains only a small percentage of the library's total holdings. If possible, embed pop-up polls on the test site asking for user feedback. This will further serve to remind users that it is only in the preliminary phase. You can also add an additional pop up to thank them for looking at the beta location, ask for their thoughts, and give links to the full catalog/databases for a more complete search.

Table 3.1 Pros and Cons of Public Release of Beta Version

Pros	Cons
Public feels that they are part of the process.	Project is incomplete. Parts of the setup aren't in final stages and feedback dwells on the incomplete sections.
Public receives full disclosure of the change that is about to take place.	Limited catalog/database entries are entered. User looks for their "go-to" book/article and it is not there.
There is a chance for feedback from a large audience.	Users assume the beta version is complete and stop using the full library sources.
	Users may bookmark the URL and continue to use it instead of the final, finished product.

If you decided not to launch your beta site publicly, consider sending the beta link to previous focus group participants or known library "super users," and ask them for their feedback. Another way to gather feedback from a subset of patrons is to broadcast the beta site from your social media outlets.

System Deployment

How will you rollout the discovery system on your library-based computers? Consider your current user experience with the library computers. Do the computers open to the desktop with an icon field? If so, is there an icon designated as a shortcut for your library web page or catalog? Does the user encounter your web page automatically when signing into the system? Does each web browser default to your library web page? If you have been effectively leading your on-site users to the main library web page, should you now refocus your efforts on introducing them to your discovery site landing page? If you are promoting this system as "one-stop shopping," then you should be directing them to the grocery store.

The argument can be made that the library user needs access to the main website for information beyond the discovery system. Before deciding how to implement your system, take time to look at your main website and your analytics to see if this is really true. The odds are very good that the greatest number of page hits on your website is for things that a user in your physical library has already figured out. Directions/map? That goes without saying. Hours? They are already there during operating hours and opening/closing times are posted near the door. Staff? Staff are probably visible from the library computers. With these items covered, your library users are probably accessing the computers to find library materials, and that is reason enough to lead them directly to the discovery system. If access to the main website is still needed, it is easy to create a desktop shortcut to the page or post small signs in the computer area with the library's URL.

Transition Planning

You have invested significant time, effort, and especially money into implementing your discovery system. How long should you continue promoting the discovery system and your library catalog/databases equally? You purchased the system for its ease of use and for it to be a one-stop shopping resource for your library. Will your users even try it if the old familiar library catalog/database links are still front and center on your web page? There are several theories on implementation:

Rip Off the Band-Aid

This method proposes implementing your discovery system by eliminating links to the other individual sources (catalog/databases) and focusing solely on the discovery system's search box. Out with the old, in with the new. The theory behind this method is that if there are no other choices, the user will have to try the new system. This is a bold move, and if you decide to pursue this path, be ready to expect pushback from your colleagues, staff, and your patrons. Be sure that frontline personnel are aware of the upcoming change, and encourage them to take the time to highlight the benefits of the new system if they receive complaints from patrons. If you take this approach, your users should be given ample warning that a big change is coming. Make sure that signage in your library and on your website has been counting down to the big reveal. If at all possible, try to launch your new system during a noncrucial time of the year, such as beginning of a new school semester or marking period, after a summer reading program in a public library, so that your patrons don't need to scramble to learn a new system during a high pressure time of year such as midterms or finals week. While there may be initial backlash over the disappearance of the catalog/databases, patrons do tend to be resilient and it isn't long before the discovery system is accepted as the "new norm."

Old and New Coexisting

This method requires the least amount of web design work. In this case, you'd simply add the discovery system search box to your library web page, and keep the traditional catalog and database links exactly as they were prior to your discovery system implementation with the same wording, font size, and location. This method is the easiest on your frontline staff because it is the least disruptive for your patrons. It should result in zero complaints from users wed to the "old" links, and will only bring on inquiries about the new search box from curious patrons. There are some very valid reasons for choosing to use this implementation method. For example, your patrons might be overwhelmed with the number of results that appear in a discovery system search, your catalog link may still be the quickest way to locate your local holdings if someone just wants to find a book or DVD. Also, some discovery systems group some formats together, for example eBooks with print books, and it may be that your local catalog is the only way to limit by a specific format. If you adopt this method, do not be surprised if users continue to fall back on the tried and true. Conduct frequent usability tests and watch the system analytics to make sure that your user numbers can justify the discovery system purchase.

Slow Fade

Some library system administrators and web designers decide to design their discovery system launch so that the discovery system search box and the traditional catalog/database links coexist on the website, but the new discovery system search box takes up more site real estate. In order for this method to be successful, the new search box must be given a prominent position on the web page with all color, graphic, and font presentation leading the user to realize that this should be the starting point of their library research journey. The theory behind this method is that your eyes and, consequently, your mind will be drawn to the bold visual representation of the search box and less attracted to the familiar old links.

If you decide to follow this method, you can display your traditional catalog and databases with their original wording, but you should make their font size significantly smaller than that used in the discovery search area. Other changes can also be made to the "old" links:

• They can be moved to a less prominent position on the page, even past the first fold if you so desire.
• You can also make the "old" links look less like links by removing underlining or making their link color match that of unlinked text.
• Place them in a list of links with other website options, instead of allowing them to stand alone.

The hybrid method is designed to not only give your discovery system a chance to shine, but also gives your frontline staff the opportunity to say, "The catalog link is still here," when dealing with patron complaints. Over time, you can slowly decrease the font size for these links, and you can move around the website, making them less prominent. Eventually, you can even move them into a dropdown menu from the main page or completely remove them. Before making the decision to gradually eliminate the "old" links, it is best to do some usability testing to see if a significant number of users are still dependent on the old tried and true.

SEARCH ENGINE OPTIMIZATION

There is a very good chance that your users are finding their way to your discovery system via search engine results. When you're studying how the patrons are finding you, take the time to conduct a variety of searches on all of the major search engines. Remember, even if your library computers default to one preferred search engine, your users may use any search engine from their home computer or mobile devices. Start with the most obvious choices:

• "search" + your library name
• the branding name of the discovery system (e.g., OwlSearch)
• "catalog" + library name
• "find book" + library name
• "book" + library name

You may be surprised to see the results that you get.

For additional possibilities, look at the external search referrers in your analytics report and reenact some of the more unusual search terms. If the search engines are not leading users consistently to your landing page, there are steps you can take to correct that. There is a science (though some may consider it an art) to Search Engine Optimization. One quick way to direct more users to your landing page is by analyzing the metadata on that page. With your new knowledge of user-preferred search terminology, you should be able to add a significant number of new keywords to your metadata to make it more robust and more noticeable to search engines.

Discovery system help features, like all help features, are best when they specifically address common issues that may arise at a particular point in the website. Some online instruction might also be helpful with a short online tutorial, or even the ? or *i* information icon strategically placed to open a window with additional directions. Also, don't forget your FAQ page. This may be an ideal question/answer entry for those users looking for some self-help. Another solution is point-of-need reference service through an ever-present button or pop-up widget for "ask a librarian" chat help.

System help features can be useful, but nothing beats a full library instruction session for helping patrons figure out the most efficient ways to use your discovery system. Not all problems can be resolved by changing your platform or web pages. As we'll see in the next chapter, sometimes the best way to resolve problems that you found by doing usability testing is to improve the ways that you teach your patrons about the system.

Chapter 4

Library Instruction and Discovery Systems

Library instruction can make a crucial impact on how widely your discovery system is used and on how well it is used by your patrons. You can never reach all your patrons through instruction. In the public library, only a subset of your patrons will attend instructional sessions. In schools and colleges, not all teachers will bring their classes to the library for instruction, and even if they all wanted instruction, there wouldn't be enough library staff to be able to teach every class and every student. But, if you can convince some of your patrons that the discovery system is a good tool to use for research, they'll tell their friends, who'll tell their friends, and your investment in the discovery system will pay off.

Library instruction can't fix all the problems that you might find when you do your usability testing, but it can help alleviate some of the issues, especially those findings where some participants were able to easily complete a task and others were not. If you found that some tasks were more difficult for some participants but not for others, consider notifying your instruction librarians and asking them to cover this particular task in their instruction sessions.

If you found in your heat mapping testing that your classic catalog links and database links were being used more heavily than your discovery system, it's worth asking your instruction librarians about how they teach their classes about the library's discovery system. Do they start their classroom or workshop instruction at the discovery system landing page? Do they show multiple ways to access the landing page from other sites? Do they emphasize the URL or easy ways to remember the URL? Are the students given any takeaways (help sheets, promotional items) with the landing page URL? This is a case where repetition matters and all the detailed instruction on internal searching do not matter if the student cannot remember how to initially access the discovery system. There are certainly cases where the traditional catalog or a single database would best fit the patron's research needs, but if even one librarian is focusing exclusively on the catalog and databases, it can greatly skew your usability results.

INSTRUCTION METHODS

Implementation of a discovery system at your library will have a big impact on how your instruction librarians do their jobs. A single-search box will be familiar to most of your patrons, and most of them will be able to come up with a decent keyword search that will get them a huge variety and number of results. The problem for your patrons will then become how to narrow or limit their searching and results to find the exact information that they need. The difference in library instruction before and after the implementation of a discovery system can be summarized as changing the skillset from *searching* to *limiting*. This can be a significant intellectual shift for many of us in the library field, because the search has been the bread and butter of librarianship since the field began. Whether we admit it or not, many of us entered this field because of a strong desire to unleash our inner Nancy Drew or Hardy Boy. The thrill is in the hunt and nothing intrigues us more than hearing "I've searched everywhere but can't find anything on _____."

Traditional library searches required browsing tables of contents for promising article titles, scanning volumes of paper indexes (oh, *Reader's Guide to Periodicals*, how you kept us busy), frantically typed elaborately constructed searches on subscription database services like Dialog that charged by the minute, all of which eventually evolved, thankfully, into searches on individual databases. Our role in our patron's research has become less about being the "keeper of the tools," like indexes or subscription searches, and more about helping our patrons be better searchers with tools that they can now access on their own. The new discovery layers we are adding in our libraries are much improved from old methods of library research, but still require instruction in some form or another. Our roles are changing, but we're still necessary to help our patrons learn to plan a search, and then decipher the results that they get.

Learning Outcomes

If you work in a college or university library, chances are good that you've been exposed to the concept of learning outcomes in one form or another. In an attempt to strive for consistency and accountability across the curriculum, most colleges require each course taught to be paired with a set of student learning outcomes. These learning outcomes provide a tool to measure whether or not the students have learned the concepts that the college planned for them to learn. Along with course-level student learning outcomes, many colleges also create program-level student learning outcomes, institutional-level student learning outcomes, and general education student learning outcomes. All these are usually tied to the college's mission statement, and the college's institutional research office or other body can use them to assess how well the college is doing at meeting their student learning goals.

In light of the widespread culture of assessment in higher education, it's a good idea to think about creating student learning outcomes for your college-level library instruction classes. You may already have goals in mind for your class, but it can be useful to spell them out for each session, so that the students know what will be expected of them and so that you can measure your effectiveness as an instructor. There are plenty of online examples of library instruction learning outcomes (Germanna Libraries, 2016). Here are a few that we've modified to use when teaching students how to use library discovery systems:

- Students will be able to create effective searches using the library's discovery system
- Students will able to fine-tune these searches by using the limiters and sorting functionality in the library's discovery system
- Students will be able to judge the credibility of a source found in the library's discovery system
- Students will be able to create a citation based on content found in the library's discovery system
- Students will be able to identify technological roadblocks in research and find ways to move past them

Where to Start

A best practice for any information literacy instruction is to start the session with a few definitions. Because we are familiar with terms like "catalog" and "database," it can be easy to forget that these words may not mean anything to our patrons. Or the words may have a non-library connotation that doesn't make sense to our patrons in the library milieu. Before you jump into talking about your discovery system, take a few minutes to talk about common library terms. Start with the concepts of "database" and "catalog" and work up to explaining how they work in the discovery system framework. If you have a brand name for your discovery system, make sure you introduce it at this time and explain that you will be using the two terms interchangeably. While explaining what a discovery system "is," it is also a good opportunity to explain what it "is not." Use this time to detail the differences between information from paid subscription databases and the Internet at large. Now is a good time to reinforce that the discovery system is not a library site search and that it's meant to provide your patrons with research sources, not things like the name of your library director, whether or not you have study rooms, and so forth.

As you go through your lesson, keep in mind that there may be other terms that you cover that may be unfamiliar to your patrons. It can be surprising to realize how many of your patrons don't recognize the word "abstract" when used in reference to the parts of an article (Imler and Eichelberger, 2014). The term "pdf" has become more widely used over the past five years, but it may still be unfamiliar as an indication that the whole article is available in a results list. The same is true for the term "html full text." Some of the symbols used in the discovery system may also be unrecognizable to your patrons. It can be a bit disheartening to realize that the tiny hard disk symbol used for "save" is completely foreign to younger students, who've never seen anything other than USB sticks used for file storage.

Keyword vs. Subject Searching

Although the focus of discovery system instruction should be how to limit your searches post-search, it's still worth your time to go over some basic search methods with your patrons. Because most for-profit search engines make it easy to find results even with natural language searches like "where is the nearest gas station?," you'll need to inform your patrons that your discovery system is not sophisticated enough to handle searches like this. A quick browse through the search box analytics on most any discovery system or library website search will bring up an alarming number of search strings beginning with "I need . . . " This is proof that there is still a need for instruction and a need for the teaching of basic search strategies. Pair your bad news about natural language searching with the fact that the results will be worth the effort to find them, because they're coming from legitimate, reviewed sources, which will be more highly regarded by their teachers and professors than Internet search results. Once you explain the nature of single word or phrase searching, your patrons should be able to come up with some basic searches that will work in the discovery system.

Another point to cover, which seems obvious to us but often escapes our patrons, is that the discovery system, like all our library systems, is very literal. Google is a lot more forgiving of poorly worded or misspelled searches than our systems. Patrons are often confused when they get zero results for a search that seems obvious to them, but because of the way it's phrased or punctuated, it's unable to be processed by our system. You'll need to remind them that the search is a computer and it's trying to match exactly what they type with the content in its collection. If they add a ? to their search, the computer will look for that ? in the books and articles in its repository. If they misspell a word or add a dash between words, such as "web-site," they need to understand that they will only get results for materials where the word was spelled that exact way.

Should you address the differences between keyword vs. subject searching, which one has long been a standard part of library instruction? Keyword searching is the basis for discovery searches and frankly is not something that needs to be taught, except as described in the previous paragraph. A basic keyword search will bring up an ample number of sources, and while they may not be the "best" sources, they will often lead the user to the correct subject terms. Subject searching as a starting point has gone out of fashion in the library world, mainly because it's so difficult to identify the correct subject terminology without first doing some general keyword searching to see what kind of results are available. It's worthwhile to explain to your patrons that a subject heading is a great way to link to other materials on the same topic, but it's better to use a keyword search to find a good article, then link out from the subject headings associated with that article rather than trying to figure out the exact structure of the subject heading before searching.

Keep in mind that your patrons are probably used to searching in Google, which helps a user through the search process with "did you mean" pop-ups that correct spelling or reword the search phrasing. Google searches also provide keyword combinations used by other searchers at the bottom of the results list, so that the current searcher can consider using a different phrase to refine their search. Discovery systems can offer similar services, and it is worthwhile to point out these areas in an instruction session. These services may not be available at the point of search like in Google, but synonyms and search suggestions can be set up to show in your results list. Showing your patrons where they can find synonyms and search suggestions after their search is more practical than trying to get them to identify a formal subject heading before they begin.

The search suggestions that appear on some discovery system results lists show additional terms linked to the original search term by other users, similar to the aforementioned Google suggestions area. This can help the user come up with new keywords that they can use to fine-tune a search, and it is especially helpful when they are unfamiliar with the topic and its nuances. However, it should be pointed out that when a search term appears in the suggestions section, it is a sign of frequent use by previous searchers, and is not necessarily the best phrase combination to use nor is it true subject headings. The search suggestions are only as accurate as the previous searchers' grasp of the subject and ability to form a good search. To find the official subject headings associated with an item on the results list, the researcher will need to delve deeper than that initial list of results. It's useful to show your class how to look for subject headings within the full item record of a citation on their results list. The subject headings can also be found in some discovery systems clicking on a *more details* link near the citation. If it seems to you and your instruction librarians that subject headings are less prominent in the discovery system than they were in previous library automation products, it is by design. Keyword searching has become the norm for our users in other Internet settings, and with full document keyword searching, it has become less and less necessary to push subject exactitude.

Advanced Search

All the discovery system platforms offer an advanced search along with the basic keyword search. You may have investigated this search when you were making decisions about how to design your discovery system search box and other entry points. The advanced search gives the experienced researcher the opportunity to combine multiple types of searches such as title, author, and publication source. It also gives the user the ability to limit their search before they begin their search rather than the basic search which lets them limit from the results screen. Standard advanced search options include limits for full text, peer-reviewed journals, data ranges, language, and other more specialized limiters that you may have activated when setting up your system such as "available in library collection" or materials from a particular local collection.

While the advanced search is handy for the experienced researcher, teaching your students how to use it in a general library instruction class is up for debate. Some instruction librarians like to teach their classes how to use the advanced search because they believe that it prepares students to become master researchers. However, advanced searching, as opposed to basic keyword searching, tends to defeat the "easy to use, easy to navigate" discovery system purpose. The advanced search is most often needed and appreciated when there is a known search, or when the researcher is familiar with the structure of databases and how they work. When the user wants a particular citation instead of just anything on the topic, the advanced search can be their best friend. For that reason, teaching the advanced search is most appropriate for upper level undergraduates, graduate students, and faculty, and it should be avoided when teaching discovery system searching to public library patrons, novice researchers, and general library instruction classes.

Boolean Quotation Marks and Truncation

While it's best to stick to the basic keyword search when teaching most people about the discovery system, and to avoid getting too complicated and "librarian-like" when teaching the advanced search, it's still worth teaching your class about the classic database/catalog search tools. Boolean searching has been an essential staple in library instruction since the advent of the automated catalog and databases. While most librarians have placed equal emphasis on AND, OR, and NOT in their instruction sessions, truthfully, AND has always been the mostly widely practiced operator. The beauty of discovery systems is that they make life easier for the general researcher by defaulting to search individual words as if there was an AND between them, rather than searching the group of words together as a phrase. This mirrors the way that Google searches, and it's a vast improvement over previous databases that took each search literally and searched unconnected words as phrases. The novice searcher will have a much better chance of getting good results in the discovery system because of the assumed AND between their terms.

While the assumed AND is a great thing, your instruction session students can also benefit from learning how to group their terms into clumps, which will result in a more targeted search and will drastically decrease the often mind-blowing number of results. Like many of your stand-alone databases and many non-library search sites like Google, the discovery system lets researchers turn a clump of words into a phrase search if you add quotation marks around the phrase. For students who are unfamiliar with this trick of the trade, this can seem like a librarian superpower. When asked to list one new thing learned as a post-class assessment, students at Penn State Altoona frequently list the "quotation mark thing." The best way to teach this concept to your students is to present them with two searches: for the first search, show them the results for a search for a common phrase without quotes, and then add the quotes and show them how drastically the results change. Here's an example:

> Search for Miami Dolphins without quotations. When performed in the Genesee Community College EDS, this search resulted in 320,317 items. The results include resources about the football team, but will also include articles about real dolphins near Miami, such as "Historical Evidence of Tursiops truncatus Exhibiting Habitat Preference and Seasonal Fidelity in Northeast Florida" by Marthajane Caldwell in *Aquatic Mammals*, and materials like an essay called "Chasing Arrows" by Alia Volz in the *New England Review*.
>
> Now, add quotes in order to search "Miami Dolphins" as a phrase. Adding the quotes drops the results count to 191,554, which is slightly more than half of the previous search, and it shifts the focus of the results to the Miami Dolphins football team. It's still too many results to easily parse, but this phrase searching demonstration can be a jumping-off point to show your class how to add additional phrases to this search such as the name of a player like "Lamar Miller" or the name of the stadium "Sun Life."

Truncation is another library instruction staple that has served us well over the years. Students are often amazed to see that adding a * or # to a word will let them find all the variants that they need for their search, without listing all of them separately. A prime example of this search strategy is to show your students the difference between searching for the word teacher as one of your search terms, and then changing that to teach*, which will give you results for the word teacher, teachers, and teaching. When the phrase "teacher salary" was searched in the Genesee Community College EDS, there were 42,045 results. Adding the asterisk to the word teacher changed the result number to 56,707.

Teaching discovery system truncation can be somewhat problematic because it will increase your number of results, which are already much bigger than searching in the traditional catalog or stand-alone database, instead of limiting them to a more manageable results list. However, truncation still has its place, and its inclusion in instruction will largely be determined by

the course content. For example, education students should know that child*
and teen* are going to give them more complete search results than searching
for children and teens. It's good to briefly cover how truncation works, but
if your students do not need to do an exhaustive search for their topic, it
can be helpful to remind them that sometimes "less is more," and instead of
expanding their search by using truncation, they might be better off starting
with a simple keyword search. A final point, somewhat related to truncation,
is that students are often tempted to add a plural "s" to their keywords. If you
see that happening in your classes, it's a good idea to encourage your students
to start with the singular version of their keywords, and if they don't get the
kinds of results that they want, then move on to try adding an "s" or truncat-
ing their term.

Teaching to Limit

At first glance, the Google-like search bar of a discovery system seems like it
requires no library instruction. There's a box. You put stuff in it. It comes up
with results. After all, even a misspelled search term in a discovery system will
likely bring up at least 2,000 hits. Not necessarily good hits, but hits none-
theless. It's a given that a user will find something in the discovery system.
However, it's less likely that they will find exactly what they want or need, and
that is where library instruction comes in.

As we discussed in Chapter 3, you have control over how many databases
and other resources you choose to include in your discovery system, and those
choices can greatly impact the number of results that your patrons see after
a search. The more content you added, the larger the quantity of searchable
materials, and therefore more opportunities for high result list counts. However, whether your search commonly brings up 65, 650, 6,500, or 65,000
hits, two things are certain—this is more than the user was expecting and the
user will most likely only look at the first 10–14 results on the screen.

Usability studies and field experience shows us that the odds are slim that
the user will investigate past the first page of results, and many will not use
the scroll bar to navigate past what is referred to in web development as "the
first fold." Google uses a mystical algorithm that combines the newest content with the most relevant site, interlaced with the history of our past search
results, and using Google to find information has left our patrons with an
expectation that the first hits returned from any search will always be the best.
Our library users, expecting the same practically telepathic search algorithm
will tend to be disappointed with their discovery system results. This is why
it's crucial to teach your patrons how to limit their searches.

Default Result Ranking and Search Parameters

When you start looking at limiters in the discovery system, the first thing to
talk about with your class is relevancy ranking. As we discussed in Chapter 3,

your library can choose the default relevancy ranking for their discovery system searches, but even though you present a suggested ranking, your patrons will still have the option to change the ranking for themselves. Take time during your instruction session to point out the default search result parameters and how your patrons can change them. Most discovery systems offer a choice in result ranking between relevancy or currency (newest, oldest), but not a combination of the two.

Relevancy seems like it would make the most sense as the default search result sorting mechanism, since you don't care about new articles if they're not relevant to your topic. However, changes in the way that print content has been added to databases can make date ranges more crucial to your results sorting order. When mass digitization of print materials first started, many periodical vendors made the decision to start the digitization process with the most current edition and scan back issues, as time and resources permitted. For that reason, database searching in the late 1990s and early 2000s tended to retrieve full-text articles from the most recent decades regardless of results ranking choices, because there was a limited range of electronic data available for each journal title. As preservation of library special collections (including historic collections) has ramped up, the results list from a discovery search may include items hundreds of years old, meaning that your patrons may be surprised to see that their top-ranked results for relevancy may be much older than they expect.

While the relevance ranking toolbar can only offer you an either/or choice for relevancy and date sorting, you can show your students how to get around this dilemma by combining relevancy ranking with the date range limiter. If your library has decided to sort your discovery system search results by relevancy ranking, you can leave the ranking sort as is, and then show your students how to use the date limiter to change the size and focus of their results list. If your library sorts their results list by currency, you'll just need to switch that default to relevancy for this demonstration. Summon and EDS both provide a place to enter a start date and an end date for date limiting, either as a typed entry or by using the sliding scale to choose your dates. In Summon, you should also be able to see a bar graph showing the distribution of articles published on the topic over a certain period of time. You'll want to explain to your class that if they limit by both years and the relevancy sorting, they will get more streamlined results for their research query.

A good, solid sample search can be the best way to illustrate the importance of publication date and relevancy to your students. Here's a fun one that author Bonnie Imler uses in library instruction classes for agriculture students at Penn State Altoona:

- Students are told to create a Boolean keyword search for manure AND smell.
- The search brings up a considerable number of articles, and a first glance at the titles of the first five results on the list look promising.

- Students are asked if they would use the articles in a paper, which usually results in many nods in the room.
- Students are then asked to take a closer look at the date of publication, at which point the instructor watches in amusement as their eyes widen when they realize all the top hits were published during the Civil War era.
- Finally, the students are shown how to add a date limit for the past 20 years, which shifts the focus of the results from the smell of manure as a social concern to smell and liquid manure tanks, a more modern conundrum.

This search is interesting to most agriculture students because it ties a current farming issue, manure disposal, to the same problem in the past. [Fun fact: During the Civil War era, the large number of horses used for transportation, combined with livestock roaming loose through the streets, made the smell of manure a hot-button topic at that time. Students can clearly see the difference between relevancy ranking and date ranking through this example.]

Here are a couple more date range + relevancy teaching examples:

Pick a controversial topic. Have students conduct three searches on this topic, and ask them to limit each search to sources written during three different decades, so that they can see how the tone of the articles changes over time, as evident by their titles.

Pick a topic that has always loomed large in your students' lifetimes but wasn't a prominent topic in earlier decades (e.g., Organic Foods), and have them search for results during the current time period and in previous decades. Ask them to compare the number of results, the tone of the results, and the content.

Limiting by Format or Source Type

The limit by format or source type feature on your discovery interface should be one of its most prominent features, but it can be challenging to teach, particularly if your class is filled with students who have never used any print publication beyond a book. While major divisions in format is the one known variable that users, both students and the general public, tend to come to the library knowing:

I need a *book* by Smith.
I need five *journal articles* on steroid use.
I need a *video* about Malcolm X.

Things start to get a bit trickier when you try to explain the difference between a magazine article, a newspaper article, a blog, a journal article, a web page, and so on. To many students, these are all just words on a screen, and it is not intuitive for them to be able to tell them apart. You can tell if your patrons understand the way to limit by format by including questions about this feature in your usability testing.

Teaching format was a staple of library instruction long before the discovery system was even a glimmer in the vendors' eyes. Defining the differences between newspapers, magazines, and journals was a challenge when teaching from a print bibliography and it continues to deserve attention, although it can be problematic because many students do not ever interact with these sources in the print medium and may not understand that there are different formats, or why they should care. Gone are the days of show and tell with the long, flimsy newspaper, the glossy magazine with its flashy catch lines, and the boring journal with its drab cover and lack of advertisements. Librarians need to be more creative than ever to explain the differences in source validity and importance and why it matters, when everything just looks the same to our students.

Some of the terms listed in your limit by format will be immediately recognizable to your patrons, such as books or audiobooks or videos, and your patrons may already feel comfortable using these limits to narrow their searches. They are likely to know upfront the type of material that they want, whether it's a book, a CD, DVD, or an article, and if the article needs to be academic or not. Unfortunately, librarians do not always have control over the terminology that the vendor uses in the format or source type limit area. Given the chance, a librarian would likely name the fields with names familiar to their patrons, but unfortunately many of these options are locked in by the discovery system vendor. For example, a user looking for a DVD may struggle to locate and select the category marked "video materials." This is made even more difficult if the format list is alphabetical and it requires clicking on a *More . . .* link to display all the options. In your library instruction session, it is important to point out the differences in format type terminology and to explain how to see the full list of options if it is not readily available. You can use this teaching moment opportunity to define the term "periodical," if article formats on your list are not broken down into "magazine," "newspaper," and "journal," and you should also note if books and eBooks are lumped into the same format category.

One way to quickly alert your patrons to different format types is to check and see if your discovery system lets you activate image icons to identify the type of each item that comes up in your result list. The inclusion of a highly recognizable icon next to the format name can offer an important visual clue to help your users easily identify the type of the item. Both EDS and Summon let librarians decide whether or not they want to activate format icons in the results list, and a quick glance at the results screen will frequently show a nice mix of books, online resources, videos, and newspaper articles.

In order to help students become better researchers and help them to meet the requirements of their instructors, librarians need to emphasize which formats are acceptable for student assignments. If instructors want to see certain format types in their students' bibliographies, then they must identify those formats in their assignment descriptions. Sometimes, it's worthwhile to offer a brief overview of format options to faculty, who are reluctant to accept web resources as legitimate research paper sources because of their concerns about web data authenticity and poor sources. Younger faculty, who use databases and discovery systems for their own research, have a better understanding of the distinction between a good web resource or articles found via the discovery system and a website like Wikipedia.

One of the handy ways that discovery systems try to help students find scholarly content is by offering a "peer review" checkbox limiter. The act of limiting to peer review can now be as easy as checking a format box for the user. However, this does nothing to help the patron if they don't know what "peer review" means. It is worth taking instruction time to explain what peer review is, why it's important to scholarship, and all the different ways their instructors might refer to it, including "academic journal articles" and "scholarly articles." To fully capture students' attention, be sure to give a real-world example of scholarship gone wrong (e.g., cold fusion in a mayonnaise jar, famous cases of music copyright violation, plagiarism in political speeches, etc.) and the fallout that ensues, including tenure revoked, editors fired, and journal reputations marred. This lesson has the additional bonus of giving students a clearer view of academic life and the process that their professors need to adhere to in order to publish a research article. This also lets students see their instructors as the subject experts in their fields that they really are, and emphasizes that plagiarism is plagiarism at any level.

In Summon, your system administrator can choose to activate limiter categories for both "peer reviewed" and "scholarly and peer reviewed." If your location has chosen to do this, you'll need to explain to your library instruction class that "peer reviewed" retrieves just journal articles and "scholarly and peer reviewed" includes both journal articles and book chapters from academic books. To demonstrate this difference, you can open two windows on your display screen, one with the results of just peer review and one with scholarly and peer review, and ask the students to determine the difference between the number of results for each search and the difference in citation types.

Additional Limits

Date, format type, and relevancy are the most import limits to cover in your library instruction session, but there are many other limits that you may decide to cover, depending on the kind of class you plan to teach, and also on the number and type of limits that you discovery system administrator activated in your system. EDS offers you the ability to limit your results lists by subject, ranging from broad areas like fiction vs. nonfiction to more specific subjects pulled from the results themselves. For example, a search in the Genesee Community College EDS for trees shows the following top-ranked subject limiters in the left-hand side of the screen: research (93,643 results), forests and forestry (64,986 results), trees (60,945), and the list goes on from there after the patron clicks on the "show more" link. You might want to show your class participants how they can narrow their result pool by clicking on these subject limiters.

Publisher and Publication

Another limiter option in EDS is the ability to refine your result list by publisher or publication. Most of your patrons won't need to limit their results to publishers like Elsevier or Taylor & Francis, but this limiter area can give them a handy snapshot of the kinds of results that they're getting because the publishers and publications are listed in rank order, with the most numerous results at the top of the list. That same tree search mentioned above, for example, shows Wiley-Blackwell as the top publisher in the results list, with 372,259 results, and *The Times*, a newspaper from the United Kingdom, as the most frequently listed publication. These lists can give you a sense of the types of results that are being pulled out in response to your search, and can give your patrons ideas about how to redesign their search to either increase or decrease results from a particular publisher or publication.

Geography and Language

An additional EDS limiter is the ability to limit your results by geography, which can be very useful to demonstrate if your library instruction students have been given an assignment to find out what people in a specific area of the world think about a particular topic. This limiter can be paired with the language limiter to help foreign language students find resources in the language that they're studying, from a particular country that speaks that language. For the aforementioned trees search in EDS, 337,075 items were published in the United States, 42,637 were published in Australia, 42,032 were published in Canada, and so on.

Limiting by language may seem self-explanatory, but teaching your students to use this limiter can help them fine-tune unmanageably high search result numbers, and it can pull out foreign language publications for patrons who are studying those languages and for non-native English speakers who would like to read results in their native language. The languages that show up on the limiter list are dependent on the types of sources that you have decided to include in your discovery system. If your library subscribes to foreign language databases and you included them in the discovery system, then you should see results for those languages when you search the system. In a small community college like Genesee Community College, where the librarians decided to limit their discovery system databases to those to which the library subscribes, the range of foreign language publications will be much smaller than that of a large University like Penn State, which needs to meet the research needs of PhD candidates and students from all over the world. In the same sample trees search in the Genesee Community College EDS, the results range from English (8,965,531 results), French (9,219 results), German (3,530 results), to Zarma at the end of the list with one result. The limiter can be used to exclude language choices as well as include them. In a particularly diverse library collection, eliminating languages outside of the user's knowledge may help to remove hundreds or even thousands of results from the initial search, and make the resulting list easier for the patron to review.

Content Provider

EDS lets the patron limit their results by content provider, which at the college level can be important to demonstrate to classes whose professors are tied to having their students use a name-brand stand-alone database for their research. College students in your instruction session may have been told by their professor that they need to JSTOR or CINAHL to find articles on their topic because the professor knows that most of the sources in those databases are peer reviewed and/or scholarly, and they're hoping to weed out some of the less scholarly sources that they've seen in previous assignment submissions from their students. Because EDS retains the name of the feeder database in the details about each item on the results list, you can use the content provider limit to extract only those results that came from the required stand-alone database. For example, the content provider list includes the following providers for the search on trees: Environment Complete (312,283 results), MEDLINE (113,901 results), Literature Resource Center (47,583 results), and ERIC (3,072 results). Selecting any of those four providers would immediately change the type of material on the results list from environmental aspects of trees to the way that the word tree is used in medicine, to trees in literature, to trees in education. Your students may not be aware of the focus of each of the different databases that show up on the content provider list, but if their professor told them to use CINAHL or MEDLINE for their research, they'll be able to easily pick out those names from the list.

Library Holdings

Both EDS and Summon let library discovery system administrators choose whether or not they want to provide their patrons with the ability to search for content that is not owned by the library. The advantage to letting your patrons search everything that it's possible to search is that this will provide them with a full picture of what's available on their topic. The drawback to deciding to activate all databases and content is that you may not be able to easily get the full text of content to which you do not subscribe, and this can cause frustration for your patrons. This is especially problematic in the case of eBooks because they are not easily loaned to nonlicensed libraries via interlibrary loan (ILL).

Libraries have chosen different ways to handle the licensed vs. nonlicensed content decision. Some libraries only activate the databases to which they pay for access, making it more likely that their patrons will be able to get the full text of the content that they need. Other libraries choose to activate everything, but provide their patrons with a limit called something like "Available in Library Collection." Some libraries approach the problem from the opposite direction by activating everything, but setting up the default search to only search content in their collection, and offer an expand search checkbox on the results list. As long as all databases were initially selected during the discovery system setup, this third option lets patrons choose to open up their search to content not owned by the library, which can include brief citations from journals, databases, special collections, and repositories outside of their local library system. In the case of Summon, these entries are pulled from resources in the larger Summon library and are most always citation only, without full-text offerings. If one of your teaching goals has been to help students limit their results to a reasonable number, it is unlikely that you will want to emphasize this option. If you are working with high-level researchers, however, you will want to encourage use of this feature and include a demonstration on requesting items through the ILL service.

Teaching the Extras

The number of extras that you decide to include in your library instruction session will depend on the options that your library discovery system administration activated in the system, and the volume of information that you want to throw at your users during a single session. You will be able to make this decision based on the configuration of your system and the level of research sophistication of the participants in your instruction session. If you're teaching a group of general use community patrons or first-year students, you might want to avoid overwhelming them with information, and instead spend your time getting them up and running in the discovery system. These additional search options can greatly assist your patrons or, if used incautiously, they can muddy the waters by leading to even greater numbers of search results, and which will require your patrons to sort through unwieldy numbers of both scholarly and nonacademic sources.

Direct Links to Stand-Alone Databases

As described in Chapter 3, some discovery systems will let you choose to display links to stand-alone databases when the user types in a search term that matches keyword triggers associated with that database. For example, if your library chose to activate this option in Summon, these databases appear under the heading of "Database Recommendations" and are prominently displayed at the beginning of the results list. These databases can be helpful for specialized research because they provide the user with the option to switch their search activity to a subject-curated collection of resources. However, clicking on the database link immediately takes the user to an unfamiliar interface and requires them to redo their search. During instruction, you will want to explain why these databases appear on some searches but not others, and expand on why you might want to use these links for advanced research.

Research Guides

Some systems can also let you choose whether or not you want your research guides to appear on the results screen, as long as the patron's search matches with predefined search terms. In Summon, these guides appear in boxes on the right-hand side of the screen marked "Recommended Research Guides." In EDS, you can set your research guides up as a widget that can appear in the right-hand column of the screen. Adding your research guides to your discovery system can help promote content that you may have created on platforms like Springshare's LibGuides, and increase their visibility and use. These links can direct your patrons to course-specific information, subject specialist librarian contact details, as well as additional web or print resources. If you decide to cover this topic during your instruction session, be sure to show your students all the sources that they can find from clicking on this single link. Like the direct links to stand-alone databases, these research guides often are set up to open in a new window each time the patrons click on the link. It is important to demonstrate how to get back to main discovery system pages after clicking out on these special resource links. Your patrons can sometimes be confused by layers of windows that need to be closed out before they see their original starting point.

Subject Librarian Links

Summon lets library staff decide whether or not to provide a direct link to a librarian who specializes in the subject searched by the user, without requiring the user to sort through the library staff directory. Librarians are selected based on their subject specialties and how they correspond to the search term entered. Normally, only the broadest of search terms, such as "Biology," "Agriculture," or "Nursing," trigger a "Suggested Librarian" box to appear. Most librarian entries include a photo, name, and e-mail address. These links can be especially helpful for students involved in upper level research, and they can be a good way for librarians to promote their subject-searching skills and willingness to help students with their assignments.

Reference Sources

Depending on your system's options, your site administrator may have decided to include search topic definitions from your licensed online reference sources such as dictionaries, encyclopedias, handbooks from sources such as Credo or Gale Virtual Reference Library, or from Wikipedia. It is at the discretion of the libraries to include any or all these sources. The inclusion or exclusion of Wikipedia provides an opportunity for lively classroom discussion. If you choose to display multiple reference sources in your discovery system results screen, this can create an easy opportunity for the Wikipedia definition to be juxtaposed with the commercial, academic definitions.

Both EDS and Summon provide the option to display reference source definitions for common research topics in special boxes on your discovery system results list. Activating this option in your discovery system setting can greatly increase the visibility and use of these reference resources, which can help to justify the increasing cost of these online materials. As physical reference collections in the library have shrunk or disappeared, it is less likely that your users are familiar with this type of academic source and the role they play in research. For that reason alone, users are unlikely to search for a reference work by title or even want to know that such resources exist. In addition, links to online reference works are often excluded from or buried on library websites. The discovery system can revitalize these sources.

Summon subscribers have the option of presenting reference entries and definitions in two formats. Reference entries may be displayed as one of many items in the results list, sharing equal footing with article and book citations. These entries, designed to be brief, will only contain minimal bibliographic detail and a link to the full text of the entry. The brevity of the citations lets the patron quickly scan a variety of sources on one screen. This type of presentation can highlight the interdisciplinary nature of the search topic, by displaying an array of reference works from a variety of subject areas. For example, the subject "music therapy" may call up definitions from reference works in psychology, medicine, music, elementary education, and gerontology.

The other online reference format in Summon is the definition box in the Topic Explorer section, which is similar to EDS's Research Starter display box. The Topic Explorer gives users the chance to enhance their research skills and search results by offering a series of window-like boxes on the right-hand side of the results screen, which appear after the patron's initial search is completed. The definitions are nicely organized—the entry either appears on the screen in its entirety or with a few opening lines and a *more* option. These definition boxes can reassure the user that the terms that they have selected are relevant to their topic, and can also provide additional keywords or subheadings that they can use to redesign and fine-tune their search.

If your discovery system administrator activated reference sources in your results list, and if you choose to include this resource in your instruction class session, this can make for a nice segue way into a discussion of the best sources to use for a research paper or report (i.e., Wikipedia = no, scholarly articles = yes) and how to cite the content that you find in the library's discovery system.

Citation

These days, both stand-alone databases and library discovery systems provide links that are intended to help patrons create bibliographic citations in standard styles like MLA and APA, which can then be copied and pasted into the patron's research paper or report. The discovery systems also offer the option to export citations into citation manager software like EasyBib, EndNote, or others. In this time of automated citation creation, it is an interesting challenge to teach the importance of correct citation methods when students can see these citation links on their search results. They need to be convinced that the system-produced citation tools are not always accurate, and they need to have a solid understanding of how citation works instead of blindly trusting the automatic citation tools, which can appear on the results list level, or at the catalog or database level.

Librarians are aware of the many pitfalls of these automated citation tools. The best way to persuade students that citation knowledge is useful is by demonstrating the problems with the tools. Here are a few things to stress:

Garbage in = Garbage out: Emphasize that the database is producing these citations from a formula and that the formula only works correctly if all the fields were entered correctly by the journal or database. Excellent "bad" examples come from those companies that submit their article titles in ALL CAPS. None of the common style formats require citations in ALL CAPS, unless it was originally published as such.

The importance of recognizing format: Trying to insert book chapter information into journal article citation fields is like trying to put a square peg in a round hole. However, this is a common error seen with automatically produced citations.

Spacing and punctuation: It is difficult for an automated system to identify the length of fields and eliminate punctuation that was accidentally included in the submitted text. This can lead to two punctuation marks at the end of a title, multiple spaces in the middle of an entry, and no indentation of second and third lines.

Double-checking with an authorized source: Use this as an opportunity to promote your institution's citation links and helpsheets. Show examples of reputable online sources and even bring copies of the print style manuals to your class, so that your students can get a sense of the amount of time and effort that's been put into creating these style guides.

Do not just cut and paste: Even after checking against an authorized source, stress the need to match font type and size with the other citations and text in the student's paper, when they decide to cut and paste a citation example from the discovery system's citation tool to their paper/report.

Discovery System Help

It would be nice to believe that the students in your library instruction class will remember everything that you told them about the discovery system, and that they will tell their friends, and that it will all come rushing back to them when the time comes for them to sit down and start their research. This is an impossibility. If the students in your class remember nothing else, try to impress upon them that there are ways for them to get help when they're ready to start searching. This help can come from the library itself in the form of in-person or virtual reference support, and you can also show them how to use the discovery system's help tools.

Promoting the Library Reference Desk

The library instruction session is a perfect place to promote your library reference desk. Make sure to encourage the students to ask questions, whether in person, by phone, text, via chat—in any way that you offer reference support at your library. Patrons can often be intimidated by librarians, which is why many academic libraries have hired student workers to answer some of the more routine questions, leaving the more complicated research queries for professional librarians. No one wants to feel stupid, and it can be difficult to approach a stranger for help, even if you desperately need it. Describe your library and your librarians as friendly, helpful people, whose job it is to help people. If you're up for a shameless plug for reference stats, you can tell your students that their questions boosts your library statistics and that they're actually helping you when they ask for help, not bothering you.

Both EDS and Summon provide multiple ways to bring your reference service into the discovery service, and it's a good idea to cover all of these ways in your instruction session. Both systems provide the opportunity for your discovery system administrator to control the look and feel of the discovery header, which is one of the places that they can add links to your library's reference desk information page or your library's online chat system. In Summon, this header area can be configured, so that it shows whether or not your online chat system is active or not and a patron can contact the chat system directly from the discovery system. Sometimes, these links and chat icons can fade into the woodwork when they're stuck in a header; so, it's a good idea to show your library instruction class where these links are located and how to use them.

Both EDS and Summon will allow a library to embed and implement a reference chat widget within the discovery system interface, including LibraryH3lp and LibAnswers. These widgets can pop up or remain as a steady presence on the side of the screen. Help widgets are starting to appear with regularity on commercial websites in order to assist customers with online ordering, so it's likely that your patrons have had some experience with this type of service. Even so, it is worthwhile to include a short demonstration of your reference chat during an instruction session. If your chat is summoned by clicking on an icon or "Ask Here" button on every web page, users may have come to ignore it as part of the white noise of your website. There is also the possibility of users being "scared" to use the chat reference for many of the same reasons some people will not approach a reference desk. Demonstrations do not have to take long and your reference question on the chat should make it clear to the person at the other end that this is a class demo. Some things to cover during the demo are live chat hours (if not 24/7), types of questions to ask, and the emphasis that a real person is at the other end of the chat. The last item is what tends to surprise student users the most. Many students at Penn State Altoona have confessed that they thought it was a computerized service.

Along with showing your students the ways that they can contact a librarian for during all of the steps of their research process in the discovery system, it's also worthwhile to show them how to use the help tools included in the discovery system. Like many other websites or software like Microsoft Office, EDS offers links to extensive help within the discovery system, and like these other products, the links to help show up as a small question mark icon contained in a circle. For example, in the advanced search menu in EDS, the question mark appears next to the search and clear buttons. If you click on it, a smaller browser window pops up and take you to the EDS how-to guide for "Advanced Search—Guide-Style Find Fields." It's helpful that this window is smaller than your original search screen because you can see the discovery system window behind the help window, and it's easy to get back to your starting point once you're done with the help.

Teaching Library Research Grit

The concept of a fully functioning discovery system seems like a dream come true for many librarians—all your catalogs and databases holding hands in a circle, working together in harmony, like an old-fashioned Coke™ commercial (Coca-Cola). We love the fact that search results and full-text resources are only a few clicks away. While those "few clicks away" may not seem like a barrier to those of us who know how to use them, they pose a barrier to our patrons, who can get easily lost in our maze of links and who might almost get to their final full-text destination but may lose steam and quit before they get there. You may have seen this phenomenon when you analyzed your usability data. If you recorded your patron behavior using screen capture technology, you may find yourself rooting for the patron to keep clicking until they reach their end goal, only to be disappointed when the confusing screens and many clicks cause your patron to give up (Imler and Eichelberger, 2011).

To understand why our students can be derailed by several mouse clicks that would only take a few seconds of time, we must take a few things into account:

1. Our students can reach their destination from a Google search in one click, and have limited patience with our more complicated discovery systems.
2. The terminology used to define the links that the student needs to click may not mean anything to them (e.g., "pdf," "html full text," "Get It").

3. Students are less likely to click on a format link and more likely to click on the longest link. For example, they are less likely to click on a link marked pdf and more likely to click on the article title, even though the article title will probably only lead them to the citation/abstract screen (Imler, Neuwirth and Wisniewski, 2014).

4. Students can become confused if they're required to pass through disjointed websites that look and feel different from their starting point, including your link resolver page and the endpoint database page, which may not even take them directly to the full text of their article, but may take them instead to a journal page or to another search box in a different database, where they'll need to redo their search.

We have all come to expect instant gratification from search engines like Google, and anything less is a letdown. Also, Google does an incredible job of weeding out broken links and 404 error messages. When was the last time you received a broken link on a Google search? Unfortunately, broken links are part of the discovery system universe and often the redirect "help" pages are less than useful, with options to redo your search in the library catalog or request the item through ILL. If the user has never used any library resource besides the discovery system, they may not know how to use either of those options.

On to point #2, library terminology. So much has been written in the literature about our patrons' confusion with library jargon, but that still hasn't stopped us from using and misusing it when creating web interfaces. The fact of the matter is that for some terms there are no synonyms and there is no way to resolve the confusion other than through instruction. Here are a few things to remember when teaching students how to get from their search results to the full text of a resource:

> If a crucial link is in the form of a button, and that button looks more like a piece of clipart than something that they would think to click, take the time to point out that it is a button. This can even be the case with a button marked with *i* for additional information, which is often recognized by librarians but not regular users.
>
> Likewise, if the link they need is not underlined or highlighted in any way (i.e., looks like regular text), point out that it's clickable (and ask your site administrator if this can be fixed to make the linking more obvious).

Another important way you can help your students is by defining your discovery system's full-text format icons and terminology. Though you may assume that everyone knows this, it is not common knowledge that pdf, html text, or the Adobe icon means the entire article. Similarly, for most students, the word abstract may only mean a type of art and not the summary of an arti cle. The definition of abstract is particularly important because if the user has to leave the discovery system via your link resolver in order to get to the full text of the article in a stand-alone database or publisher website, the website may default to display only the article's citation and abstract, and the student may be tempted to confuse the abstract for the entire article instead of searching for a pdf or full-text link. It may seem impossible to confuse a little one- or two-paragraph summary for an article, but think about how they receive their information by way of technology. Texts, blog posts, and news stories all come through their phones and tablets in small information bites of a few sentences or paragraphs.

Point #3 comes up repeatedly in usability studies, yet it defies logic. When given a choice between a short, format link or a longer link (more letters), student users tend to choose the longer link. For example, for this article from EDS, a student would be more likely to click on the title of the article "Africa's Indigenous Fruit Trees" rather than the direct html or pdf link to the full text of the article. Summon offers the patrons even more clickable links in the results list, depending on how it's been set up at your library, including the original database, links on the author's name or names, call number links, and so forth.

As a librarian, we would immediately understand that clicking on pdf or html would give us the full text of the article that we wanted. But faced with these choices and without instruction, students have no idea where to click, and will often pick the title link when they could get the full text immediately by picking the pdf or html link. Clicking on the title often takes them to an additional page with the format links, and clicking on the database name can lead them to the database search screen with no evidence at all of their original search or search terms. At this point, many users will realize that they are not in Kansas anymore and will just give up. Teaching students how to identify and access the different types of full text is necessary because it is not intuitive. Better web design could help resolve this problem, but you may have no control of this part of the discovery system.

Ways to teach research grit:
- Show follow through on at least one article from the search results page to the full text of the article.
- Show one article with a broken link. It's important to demonstrate that the system is not perfect and that they may run into roadblocks when searching.
- Teach the pros and cons of choosing html full text vs. pdf format.
- Emphasize the importance of being able to identify where they found the full text of the article, whether it was in the discovery system or if they linked out to another database or publisher site, because they'll need that information for citation purposes.

Your discovery system can be an amazing tool for researchers in your library, but while the basic search is more intuitive than those of traditional catalogs and databases, there are still many facets of the system that need to be described and explained in library instruction classes. What if you can't reach all your patrons through library instruction? It's now time to move on to promotion! Or, how to tell as many people as possible about the glory of your library discovery system.

Chapter 5

PR and Community Buy-In

In the old days, library promotion was limited to physical rather than virtual promotion such as signage, bookmarks, or posters, in-person roll-out events and word of mouth. Roll-out parties and physical materials are still part of PR—cake is always a good way to pull people into the library—but today's library PR needs to reach every potential library user and should extend to web, e-mail, and social media coverage. When you conducted your usability studies, did you find that patrons didn't even know that you had a discovery system? If so, then it's time to put some energy into beefing up your discovery system PR and work to get better buy-in for the system from your constituent groups including community patrons, students, teachers, and staff.

NAMING YOUR DISCOVERY SYSTEM

Do we really need to name and/or brand our discovery system? The answer is "yes." No matter how large a part the discovery system ultimately plays in a library's online presence, there will still be the need to distinguish it from the other offerings when you're working with patrons and when you need to discuss it with your library colleagues. In the library world, all our databases, catalogs, and special collections have names, so it makes sense to name our discovery system as well. Even if you replace all your stand-alone research tools and redesign your library homepage so that all you see is a single-search box for the discovery system, the box will still need a name, even if it's as simple as "Library Search." For better or worse, few libraries can afford to use their web real estate in this manner, and giving the discovery system a prominent location and name is needed in order to distinguish it from every other link on the web page.

The odds are good that your library staff has had little or no previous opportunity to take part in a branding project. Unless you work in a brand new library, it's likely that your library was named long ago for a generous benefactor, a local person of importance, or based on geographic location. The discovery system purchase may be your library's first chance at coming up with a brand that you would like to have become a household name in your user community. To clarify what we mean by "name" and "brand," the name that you choose will be part of the brand, but the brand will likely contain more than just the name. The brand is more of what we tend to think of a logo: the name written in a stylized way, plus a set color palette, and graphic elements. As it happens in the corporate world, your brand may be used for more than one product and you may want to coordinate your text, colors, or graphics with those that have previously been established for your institution, for programs within your library, or for special collections. It's good to have some consistency in branding so that your patrons see the library and its resources as a unified package.

What's In a Name?

The most difficult part of creating a brand name, regardless of the product, is coming up with something catchy and succinct that encapsulates what the product can do. In the case of a discovery system search, what makes it even more difficult is that this is not a physical product. A person can't glance at it and guess that it is a type of vacuum cleaner or a new chair. In addition, the idea of being able to search multiple platforms with the same search is still a relatively new concept and not one with which longstanding patrons are necessarily familiar, or would even guess is possible. On the other hand, new patrons may not understand the need for the brand name and its promotion because they may already assume that the library works like Google, with an all-encompassing search tool.

A quick review of popular discovery system names shows that most fall into a few categories:

Enhancers: If your discovery system will completely replace your online catalog and your catalog already has a branded name, many libraries incorporate the old catalog name with an enhancer term to indicate that it is the catalog with additions. Common enhancer words that are used include "plus" and "discover." For example, the State University of New York's Geneseo campus's traditional catalog was called "Glocat" and their Summon-driven discovery system search is called "Glocat+."

Local knowledge: Many libraries give their discovery system name a local flavor. It is fairly common to see brand names chosen that include the library name, town/ county name, or the local sports mascot name in combination with some form of the word "search." For example, the Penn State University discovery system name is LionSearch because the university sports teams are called the Nittany Lions.

Superlatives: Many libraries use the generic word "search" as part of their discovery system name, since that's the purpose of the discovery system, but they often add prefixes such as "mega," "extra," or "ultra" to show just how big the search is compared to the old search tools. If you have seen the term on a box of laundry detergent, it has probably been used to describe a discovery system search.

Naming Decisions

Discovery system companies provide you with a name for their system (EDS, Summon, Worldcat Local, etc.) and if you decide to keep that name, it's a nice marketing tool for those vendors. Unfortunately, these names do little to convey their potential to patrons. Another problem with keeping the vendor name is that if your patron tried to find your system by doing a Google search, the first results would be for the vendor's site, not for your specific instance of their product. Giving your discovery system a local name will make it easier for your patrons to find if they choose to look for it via a web search rather than starting at your library homepage. Most libraries choose to replace the vendor name with a local brand, at least for promotion to the public. Note that the company names do live on behind the scenes with those who selected the system and those who continue to work with it daily, so it's good for library staff to know both the public and the private names for your discovery system.

What's the best way to come up with a name for your discovery system? The local brand name idea may come from a single individual or a committee. It may be created at an organized brainstorming session or through results from a naming contest sent to staff and/or the public. Once you come up with some name options, who gets the final say in the name selection? Do you form a committee to decide? Will you let your patrons have a vote in the new name?

There are several ways to kick-start a discovery system name brainstorming session. First, decide who'll be invited to the session, and then pick a meeting date, time, and location. Set up the room so that you have a place to list name ideas such as a white board or a flip chart. You can prepopulate these lists with keywords to remind your brainstorming participants of local landmark/mascot names, searchable resources, and action verbs related to the discovery system. These lists can then be used in mix and match fashion in an attempt to create a composite name. Another method is to have the participants complete a sample discovery system search and write a description of its functionality in 25 words or less. Request that the descriptions be submitted ahead of the scheduled meeting and create a word cloud of the most widely used terms from the descriptions. The word cloud can indicate each word or phrase's popularity with differences in font size or color. This will give the committee an idea of the terms most widely associated with the new system and should aid in the creation of a name.

Another way to gather ideas for your discovery system name is to create a system naming contest and invite library staff, or patrons, or everyone to participate. All contest participants should have access to a sneak preview of the discovery system in order to help them understand what the system does, which should help them to generate appropriate names. Having a prize for the contest winner is a nice incentive, but is not always necessary for this type of contest. Because the survey takes little time or effort, many people will participate, and they will have bragging rights if their name is chosen. Contest participants do not have to be limited to in-person patrons, as basic form can be created online to accept submissions. Social media advertising can attract even more participants. Naming contests are a case where more is better—there is no need to limit individuals to only one entry.

Contest judging can be the responsibility of a committee or an administrator. It's up to you to decide what would work best at your location. Many of the submissions will be able to be quickly dismissed, but there will usually be multiple viable name candidates, and choosing one can be a difficult choice. If you are lucky enough to come up with multiple promising entries, it may be a good idea to solicit public input through a popular vote. Involving your public will help you promote the new system, and help your patrons to feel more involved in the new product, and will make them more familiar with it and more likely to use it. Creating a quick, online, pop-up poll only takes a few minutes and will quickly let you know which name resonates the most with your users. In addition to helping select the name, a contest can also give you three ways to connect with your users through personal contact, online interaction, and social media: the contest announcement when the poll of semifinalists is ready and when the final name announcement is made.

Before sending out the poll of semifinalists, it is wise to do a quick pop culture test of your potential names to see if any of them fail the test. Do a quick Internet search and run the names past users of different ages to check for possible double meanings or negative connotations. If one of the proposed names does come up frequently in the Internet search for other locations, you may want to reconsider using that name. Even if you brand successfully and your discovery search is an overwhelming success, it still might take a long time for your library site to come to the top of a search results list if there are other places using the same name. Successful branding will mean that your users will know your site name and may search for it online, and you do not want to risk losing them if they have to scroll to find your site.

Regardless of how it is chosen, you will want to promote your new name far and wide. If a contest was held to choose the name, you will want to inform the winner and other finalists that the contest is over before you release the chosen name. The new name should also be broadcast by signage in the library building and by creating multiple messages on your website and via social media. This is also the time to have an artistic member of the library staff or a hired graphic artist begin work on an "official" brand logo with the name in a specific font type, font size, color, and iconic graphic element. Much has been written about the power of branding, and it is worth the time, effort, and money to get the brand right.

For the brand to be successful, the library staff must embrace it and begin to consistently refer to the system with the new name. When they help patrons to use the system they need to say, "Let's use *insert brand name*" and "Have you tried *insert brand name*?" Constant repetition is the only way the name will catch on.

Your library staff are the best promoters of your new system. Encourage your instruction librarians to refer to the discovery system by its local name when they're teaching a class. It is easy to say "Let's start at the search box on the web page," instead of "Let's use *insert brand name*." In a library instruction session, the brand name should not only be introduced, but also defined as a way to search a multitude of sources. It should be sold as quick, easy, one-stop shopping for all your library resources. If the brand name can be worked into an instruction session three or four times, it will be more likely to click with your patrons. To assess if the branding has been effective in the classroom, include one or two questions about the discovery system in a follow-up questionnaire or post-test, and be sure to refer to it by the brand name. If students raise their hands to ask what the brand name means, it was not successfully emphasized during class. In addition to introducing the brand name in class, also be sure to include it on any printed class handouts or online course guides.

Your staff can help not only with promoting the system, but also with assessing whether or not the promotion is working. One of the easiest discovery system brand name recognition tests is to ask your frontline staff to start their reference transactions, when appropriate, with the question, "Have you already tried searching *insert brand name*?" If the patron quickly says "yes" or "no," they recognized the term. If they look confused and respond "I don't think so" or "I'm not sure what that is," then they didn't recognize it. Give your staff member a tick sheet and ask them to place a tally mark under a column marked "Recognized" or "Did Not Recognize." This test only needs to be run for about a week. The frontline staff may note that patrons responded by saying that they did "a library search." While your goal is to gain name recognition for your brand, it's not necessarily a bad thing if your patron thinks of the discovery system as the library search. In a way, it elevates your search to being closer to say a Google search in your patrons' eyes. In the authors' informal poll on a popular library listserv, librarians responded that their patrons most often refer to the discovery system search as "the library search," regardless of the name given to their system.

Name Longevity

It is natural that over time as our library staff, instruction librarians, and patrons become more comfortable with the discovery system, they are less likely to promote or notice the brand. As a result, new users are less likely to have a strong or any association with the name. While it can be disturbing to see the brand falter, you will need to check whether the staff and patrons are simply becoming more casual about the brand name, or if they're not using the system itself, which is a much bigger problem. In many cases, name recognition testing may show that your patrons may not recognize the name of the discovery system, but search analytics and user testing will show continued strong use by the patron population. In an impromptu survey of discovery system naming on an active listserv, many responders proudly shared their system name and its origins, and most also admitted that they seldom hear students refer to the given name.

If you get to a point where you decide that your name brand is no longer effective, you may choose to begin to phase it out by diminishing the size of the logo on your website or by making it less prominent. You may also choose to make the search box larger and refrain from any mention of the brand until the user reaches the results page. Completely eliminating the brand can take a long time, and it may be more trouble than its worth. You will be surprised at how many websites and online library guides make mention to it by name. It will be easiest to eliminate from library-controlled online sites, and much more difficult on sites controlled by individual librarians or faculty members. In place of links to the brand, you may wish to encourage others to replace it with a search box widget and use the title the patrons have chosen, which is simply "the library search."

DISCOVERY SYSTEM PR

Whether you're trying to generate interest in a new system or your usability testing showed you that your patrons are unaware of your current system, there are many ways to promote your discovery system.

PR Leadership

Starting a new PR campaign can feel a bit overwhelming. The first thing to do is to figure out who will take the lead on the campaign. Is there someone responsible for PR at your library? Do you have a team of people who do this kind of work? In order to ensure that your discovery system gets the visibility and use that you want it to get, you'll need to make sure that the staff who are responsible for promotion know about the system and its benefits. You can design a beautiful system, but if no one knows that it's there, your work will have been for naught and you'll be paying for a system that's not getting used.

If you don't have an official PR team in place at your location, you'll need to determine who's going to promote the system and how they're going to do it. In general, a promotion effort works best when the entire library staff is on board and supportive of the system, and when everyone at the various service points in the library is willing to tell patrons about the new system. However, the campaign will need a leader to plan and implement it. It's best to give the responsibility of discovery system promotion to an individual not fully involved in the technical implementation or updating of the system itself. You need someone who's out working with your patrons and who has good ideas about how to reach them. Promoting the system should not be a one-day, one-shot deal—it requires someone with the skills and time to put into long-range planning and follow through. Leading a project like this can benefit the leader as well as the library because the role and responsibility can justify an entry on a resume and even lead to a letter of recommendation for future employment opportunities. If you don't have a librarian or staff person who's willing and able to take on a PR project of this type, consider working with an intern, a local marketing class, local library school students, library work-study students, computer science tutors, or homeschooled high school students looking for capstone projects.

PR Methods

Once you've gotten your PR leadership in place, it's time to start working on promotional materials. Here are a few of the most commonly used techniques.

Bookmarks

A bookmark may be the only physical item a patron takes home from your library. Here are some things to consider when designing bookmarks to promote your discovery system:

Branding: If your discovery system is branded with a visual logo and/or local name, make sure these are prominent on promotional items so that users may recall them when searching in a search engine.

URL target: Does the bookmark have the URL for the discovery system landing page? If your discovery system starting page is different from your library's main website URL, which do you want to promote? Having some promotional items with one URL and some with another can send a mixed message, so it's best to choose one or the other.

QR codes: Add a QR code designed to point to whichever URL you decide to promote. A QR code adds visual interest to a bookmark, and also saves space by replacing a long text-heavy URL with an image.

Posters

When you're working on your posters, it's important to be creative because a catchy image or slogan will help to pique your patrons' curiosity about the new system. If you're having trouble coming up with an idea on your own, do a couple of Google image searches on "library discovery system promotion" and "library discovery system PR" and you'll find lots of examples of PR used at other libraries. Most libraries are happy to share their content within the library community, but it's always a good idea to ask for permission before co-opting someone else's idea, and it's also good to give attribution where possible and necessary.

You can also search social media sites like Pinterest to find ways that libraries have promoted their discovery systems. You could even check Facebook and Instagram to get an idea of the types of eye-catching memes that are popular, and then use those images as part of your marketing. If you're looking for copyright-free images to use for your marketing, Pixabay (http://www .pixabay.com) and OpenClipart (https://openclipart.org/browse) are good places to start, and sites like Fotor (http://www.fotor.com) can help you create photo collages for your promotional materials. Sites like Canva (https:// www.canva.com) can help you design classy and eye-catching posters.

Here are a couple of promotional poster ideas:

Interactive poster: Make two posters and place one on top of the other, attaching them at the top edge. Design the top layer to read "Something new and exciting is coming to our library" with an arrow and the words "Lift here" in the lower right-hand corner. The poster underneath should highlight your discovery system brand and give more details about the system and its advantages. Mount the posters near the main library service desk and ask your frontline staff to take note of the number of patrons curious enough to lift the top poster.

QR code: Another way to spark patron curiosity is to use the same "Something new" wording, along with a large QR code that leads to your discovery system. If your patrons are not particularly QR code savvy, the same poster can have tear-off tabs, each printed with the URL for the system web page, in the style of signs students make to advertise for a new roommate or to sell their books.

E-mails and/or Texts

E-mailing is one of the easiest to reach a large number of library users with a personal message. Texting can also be easy and efficient, but you must have access to cell phone numbers for your patrons, and when collecting these numbers, you'll need to give users the option to allow or prohibit text messages from the library. Promotional e-mails or texts should be sent once the new system or upgrades are in place and working well so that you don't lead your users to a system that's not yet fully functional. Because of this, your PR messages should not be sent on the day of implementation. Even if your system seems to be working smoothly, it is not wise to place the added strain of dozens of patrons clicking on the link to the system at the same time.

Here are a few pointers for composing and sending a mass e-mail or text:

Privacy: Make sure that the group message does not display any other individual's e-mail address or cell phone number. One way to do this is to use your own e-mail in the To address, and put all the other recipients in the blind copy (BCC) line.
Keep it brief: E-mail is most likely to be read if it is short, with the information separated into bullet points. You'll need to make your text notifications short enough to comply with the 160-character limit.
Link accuracy: Before sending out your patron message, make sure to test your system links by sending the message to a library staff member. You do not want

to have to follow your initial message to your patrons with an apology message providing the corrected link.

Timing: Plan for to send your e-mail or text at a time when it is most likely to be seen by your patrons. First thing in the morning, on a Friday afternoon, or right before a holiday are not good times.

SAMPLE E-MAIL

Subject: Exciting Library News

In case you missed it, the new library discovery system *insert brand name* went online yesterday. We are excited because *insert brand name*:

- Allows you to search the library catalog (books, CDs, and DVDs) and 300+ databases with **one** search!
- Gives you access to two million full-text articles and over 25,000 eBooks!
- Helps you create reading lists and formats sources in MLA and APA style for bibliographies!

. . . all this and much more.

Click here to access http://testsite.com

Questions? E-mail _____.

Countdowns

It's likely that you've already implemented a discovery system at your library, and you're reading this book in order to find ways to improve it. However, if you're still working on setting up a new system and want to get started on your PR, an electronic or library signage countdown is a good way to help both library staff and patrons become more familiar with the upcoming discovery system implementation.

There are few among us who like surprises that change our workflow. Even road construction projects are now advertised weeks in advance in the media and through electronic signage in order to brace travelers for changes in traffic patterns. In the same vein, you should also prepare your users for the implementation of a discovery system or any major change to your system. When is the best time to begin your countdown? It is important that you don't start counting too far in advance as you don't want this to turn into a long, drawn-out "100 bottles of beer on the wall" experience for your patrons. Usually, 30–45 days in advance is plenty of time, and is long enough to catch the attention of even an occasional library user. There are several ways to create a physical count-in in your library:

Create a flip chart with the numbers in reverse order and tear off a sheet each day, or Write the countdown number daily on a large black or white board, which saves paper.

To draw attention to the upcoming discovery system implementation electronically, you can post a countdown clock on your library website. There are free websites online that will create the clock for you after you answer a few questions via an easy-to-use widget.

While counting down to your discovery system is a good way to promote the upcoming changes, be careful in the way you track the coming system on social media or via patron e-mails. A physical or electronic countdown clock is nonintrusive because people can glance at it and then ignore it. However, if you post a daily countdown reminder on social media or send frequent e-mails, your countdown news can become annoying, and you might get "unfriended" and "unfollowed" in a hurry. It is far more effective on social media to give weekly updates on the progress toward the discovery system and provide teasers about its capabilities.

Website Promotion

Real estate on your main library website is precious and you don't want to waste a lot of it on advertising something that has not yet occurred. A good way to notify patrons about the upcoming system is to post a countdown clock and a small teaser prominently on the page, but rather than filling up your page with additional information about the new system, link to a separate web page to provide more details for those who are curious. Users who are sincerely interested will go the extra mile to find out more. Here are few more best practices for advertising your new system on your website:

Branding: If you have given the system a name, you should start to use the new name by introducing it on the website.
Details: When designing your separate website to explain the new system to your patrons, be sure to describe *what* it can do and not *how* it works. As librarians, we can get excited about the "how" and lose sight of the fact that our users are more interested in what the new system can do for them.
Style: It's helpful to be innovative in promoting new services to your patrons. Try to avoid using outdated "Under Construction" or "What's New" language and graphics, as web users might have seen this type of notification so many times that they have trained themselves to ignore it.

Social Networking Promotion

Done correctly, social networking can be a highly effective marketing tool. If your library does not have a Facebook or Twitter account, or if your social media sites are lackluster at best, now is the time to create some new accounts or dust off your old accounts and bask in the free promotional opportunities. In public library settings, make sure that your local media outlets, community, business, and historical sites are all aware of and receive notifications from your social media avenues. Getting these "town criers" interested and excited about your new discovery system is one of the best things that can happen promotionally. A good word from them can easily reach an additional 400–600 people instantly.

As you ramp up your social media presence, it's a good idea to extend personal invitations to influential people in traditional and social media venues asking them to join your social media sites. If you are in a college/university setting, make sure that the editors of the school newspaper, student bloggers, or editors of alumni newsletters are followers of your library sites. This is also the best time to increase your number of social media followers in general. You have something you want them to know about and you are pouring extra attention into your sites. This is the perfect time for recruiting new viewers and keeping them hooked. This is not the time to passively put up a "Like us on Facebook" sign or hand out bookmarks with "Follow us on Twitter." For a limited time (e.g., two weeks, a month), go all out and encourage users to join your social media sites while waiting at service desks, while participating in an instruction session, and so forth. Your signage can read something like "Something new and exciting is coming to the library . . . don't miss it! Join us on Facebook and Twitter." Additionally, offer an incentive (small promo item) for each person willing to join on their own device (phone, tablet) in front of a library staff person, or on a tablet or laptop kept at the service desk. It is amazing how many people will sign up on the spot if a staff member holds up a clip-on book light and says, "I can give you this if you like our site on Facebook right now." To reward loyalty, you should also give the incentive item if they can prove they have already liked your site or are willing to invite people on their friends list.

Along with encouraging your live patrons to share your social media, you should make the same plea to your virtual patrons and social media followers. Anyone familiar with social media is well aware that for every "lurker" who watches but doesn't interact, there are at least three individuals who feel they must share everything that crosses their path. Take advantage of that! Ask your followers to invite people to like or follow the library sites. Many people will likely ignore the request, but a few will take it as a directive and promptly pass it along to a whole new audience. Most people see libraries as a benefit to society, and your followers may look at promoting a library site as a good way to inform their friends about community and educational programming. It also doesn't hurt to send out an e-mail to all library employees and volunteers encouraging them to invite friends and family to join the library sites or promote library events on social media. This gentle reminder is helpful because employees are already aware of upcoming changes to the library and it might not occur to them that other people might not know about upcoming changes/improvements at the library.

A good social media marketing strategy will require creativity, continuity, monitoring, and timely response to patron interaction. One creative way to promote the discovery system is to create a virtual or real-life scavenger hunt.

You can design riddle-like clues such as "Besides the 'little, green, Martian' definition, find three other different definitions for the word alien" or "In our library, is it possible to read, watch, and listen to The Color Purple?" These clues can lead them to the brick and mortar library for answers or to any number of websites, including both the library website and other useful sites.

Another way to promote the system is to create "don't you wish" teasers posted every few days, identifying things you will actually be able to achieve with the new discovery system, which could not be accomplished before. Examples of teasers include:

- Don't you wish you could search for books and articles with just one search?
- Don't you wish your search could just magically display all the peer-reviewed journal articles on your subject?
- Don't you wish you could find DVDs on a subject with one click?

Another facet of a successful social media campaign is continuity, which means keeping your project at the forefront of your patrons' minds by sending out messages about topic every couple of days. If you employed focus groups for your usability testing, this is the absolute best time to highlight the most positive quotes from the group's participants. These brief comments can serve as the ultimate teasers: "I can't believe how fast it is" and "Who knew there was that much available" are the kind of comments that make people want to know more.

#Hashtag

Another thing that you can do to draw more attention to your discovery system is to create a hashtag to be used on your promotional materials and on your social media sites. While some people may only be familiar with hashtags as means to promote an event like a conference, concert, or movie premiere, they can actually be created for any reason at all including promoting your new or existing discovery system. Hashtags were first used in Twitter, but have since expanded to other social media sources. Facebook, Instagram, and YouTube are just a few sites that are good outlets for your newly minted hashtag. Most of these sites make your hashtag instantly linkable and allow for specific hashtag searching from their main search box. Consider tagging photos from your rollout event, screen capture images, and videos demonstrating specific discovery system features. As cataloging specialists, we librarians should be extra vigilant at tagging all our documents, images, and videos with descriptive keywords and our hashtags.

When creating a hashtag, it is important that it be memorable and not previously used for some other purpose. Here are a few tips to keep in mind when creating your hashtag:

Keep it short and sweet: Twitter only allows 140 characters per message, so you do not want your hashtag to use up one half of your allotment.

Make it memorable: If you have decided to brand your discovery system, the brand name must be included in your hashtag, even if it seems strange. (Remember the first time you heard the names Google, Yahoo, and Amazon?) If you want to include your library name, abbreviate it in the shortest way possible that it can still be recognized.

Brainstorm: Run a brainstorming session with your coworkers and come up with a short list of six to eight hashtag possibilities. Take the time to rank them in case more than one could be a viable choice. Conduct a Twitter search for the hashtag and a general Google search (both with and without the # sign) to see if there are any matches. Discard any hashtags that have ever been used before. It is not worth the aggravation or confusion of selecting a previously used hashtag.

Review suffixes: If you decide to use your brand as your hashtag, do the same Twitter and Google searches mentioned above to make sure that other versions of your tag are unique. A few common suffices, or add-ons, are "new," "event," or the current year. For example, if your hashtag is #owlsearch, make sure that any other variation of that term that you may use is unique, such as #owlsearch2016 or #owlsearchnew. Think of it as a subject heading research project.

Peer (and non-peer) review: Sometimes, in our haste to create a brief hashtag, we accidentally come up with a letter combination that means something else entirely, such as "WTF" or other not safe for work acronyms. It is a good idea to run your proposed hashtag past a diverse group of potential patrons to see if any of them react by covering their face and chuckling. You don't want your hashtag to be trending and popular for all the wrong reasons.

Your hashtag can be a big part of your discovery system PR package, but it will have zero effect if you do not actively promote the hashtag itself. Creating a hashtag and not telling anyone about it brings to mind the question about a tree falling in the woods making a noise. Here are some well-known and easy ways to promote your hashtag:

Bookmarks: It takes less than five minutes to open a new Microsoft Word document and type your hashtag in the largest font possible that will fit on one line. Copy the text and paste it five more times on the same page to produce six bookmarks on a single sheet. Print on cardstock and you have a first-class bookmark. Make sure that your frontline staff places one bookmark in one book each time a patron checks out.

Magnets: Printable, thin magnetic sheets are inexpensive and widely available for use in inkjet and laser printers. In about the same time as it takes to create a set of bookmarks, you can print your own magnets with the hashtag from a Word document. Distribute the magnets to members of your community who have access to an even larger part of your audience than you might see inside the library. In a university or elementary/high school setting, distribute the magnets to faculty members and ask them to place them on filing cabinets and magnetic whiteboards in their offices or classrooms. In a public library, you could give sets of magnets to local teachers or businesspeople and ask them to promote your new service by prominently displaying the magnet.

Banners: The cost of producing good quality vinyl and paper banners has greatly decreased in recent years. You may even have access to a large format printer on your campus or in your community. Take advantage of this to create a few large banners to promote your hashtag. You would want to display at least some of the banners in the library, but others could be placed elsewhere in the community. In a school setting, they can be placed in student lounges and cafeterias. If you can obtain permission to post them in gymnasiums or on sports fields, it will garner you even more free publicity. If you work in a public library, take some time to explore whether or not you can place the banner temporarily at local parks, the mall, or the town square. Banners will be most effective if you use bold text in a bright color on a contrasting background color. Simplicity is the best way to go. Do not clutter banners with additional text description or images.

Electronic signage: Electronic signage is everywhere today. If your library owns its own electric sign, experiment with the many different ways you can post your hashtag using different fonts, different sizes, and positive/negative backgrounds. Also, take note of other electronic signs in your area, the owners of which may be willing to provide you with space for a slide on their system. These may be in other campus buildings or other businesses in the community. It is worth asking if these other locations are willing to add your hashtag in with the rotation of their messages. Be prepared to explain what a discovery system is and why it is a big deal. You should specifically ask for a set period of time such as three days or a week. If you can convince other locations to broadcast your hashtag, you should also decide if you would like to blast your message from every location at the exact same time, or would you rather stagger its appearance over the month before the unveiling. There are valid reasons for going with either strategy.

For a hashtag to be effective, it needs to stir up curiosity in the observer—enough curiosity that they will actually take the time to investigate its meaning. If you haven't created any web-searchable content that explains what your hashtag means and why it's important, your patrons can become frustrated when they try to Google your tag in order to find more information about it. You could add this information to your stand-alone web page about the discovery system, but an even better way to track the reach of your hashtag is to create a back-end web page that describes the hashtag, and make that page only accessible via a Google search or a targeted URL rather than making it visible on your web page. You could also publicize the URL that explains the meaning of the tag as text, or you could turn it into a QR code that you could add to your bookmarks or magnets or other marketing materials. By limiting the access points to the web page, you will be able to use your website analytics to monitor the number of people who located the explanation web page by using the QR code or a hashtag search. Make sure that your hashtag explanation site is clear and concise, and that it highlights the best points of the discovery system, gives the implementation date, and invites users to any rollout events. You can even add an offer of a small promotional item on the explanation web page, letting any followers know that they can receive a small gift if they mention the hashtag on their next visit to the library.

Embedding Your Twitter Feed

Once you have established your hashtag, you can promote it and everything that's being said about it by adding the Twitter feed to your library web page. Through a combination of html and JavaScript, you can embed either a single flattering tweet on your main library website, or you can use the Twitter widget to embed a Twitter timeline, which is a list of tweets from newest to oldest on a separate social media web page. Embedded timelines allow you to display either a single Twitter account or multiple accounts. You can also set up a timeline to display the results of a Twitter search for your brand name, which can be particularly helpful if you have created multiple variations on your hashtag, but all contain your discovery system brand. Embedded timelines appear on the website as a neat column, and the code provides you with options for customized banners, column sizes, and color choices.

Monitoring Your Hashtags

It is important to monitor your hashtags to see how often and where they are being used. Analytics are available from individual social media sites like Twitter, Facebook, and more, and also from social media management sites like Hootsuite that pull your data from multiple outlets and allow you to see the big picture of your online presence. In Twitter, the Tweet activity dashboard is free to users and offers a microlevel analysis of action on your site. Unlike web analytics that measure searches and hits to their site, Twitter reports on impressions and engagements. The difference between a "hit" and an "impression" is that "hits" occur when people choose to deliberately go to a web page by typing and entering its URL, or by clicking on a search result that takes them to that page. "Impressions" occur when a tweet is pushed out to a number of users. An impression tells you that your Tweet was sent, but it does not give any indication if the Tweet was acted upon or even read.

When you create your discovery system promotional Tweets, they'll be sent out to your library Twitter followers. But your reach won't end there. If a larger feed like a college or local-interest site retweets your posts, you will also gain their followers in your impressions analytic. If individuals send on your initial tweet, their numbers will also be added into the impressions analytic. In a matter of minutes, your original tweet can potentially reach thousands of Twitter accounts. This is why encouraging your library staff to retweet your content from their personal accounts can really go a long way to boosting your output. Another way to encourage retweeting is to offer promotional items to your patrons if they agree to retweet your posts and show proof of the retweet to a library staff member.

When reviewing your analytics, the number of engagements is more important than the number of impressions. Twitter engagements appear on your activity dashboard and indicate that a tweet was read and acted upon by your readers. Twitter will provide you with the total number of engagements, and will then break down each tweet into "media engagements (clicks on a picture or video)," "Retweets," "Likes," and "Link clicks."

To analyze your hashtag beyond Twitter, you may want to investigate hashtag tracking tools such as Hashtagify and Tagboard among many others. These types of tools are often downloadable for free or for a subscription rate. Each tool offers its own features, but most will track your hashtag on multiple platforms and offer data on its trending rate. Other possible tracking options are percentages of positive, negative, and neutral posts, graphs that list other hashtags that have been associated with yours, and some sites even offer a pin board-type feature that shows you each post that was spawned from your original post.

The analytics tools presented by each individual social media outlet are likely to give you the most detailed statistics about your online interactions. However, monitoring and analyzing all these separate sites can be time consuming and labor intensive. Hashtag tracking is just one piece of your social media analytics pie, and for that reason, vendors have created social media dashboards like Hootsuite or Sendible. Social media dashboards can track interactions on all your library sites in real time and show you the results on one screen. Most social media dashboards offer a free trial run, but few are truly free. Expect to pay either a monthly/yearly subscription fee, or "pay to play" by selecting from an à la carte list of individual widgets, apps, and other enhancement features. These sites track not only individual stats for each media outlet, but also calculate the effectiveness of your overall social media efforts, creating ready-made graphs and charts that you can include in presentations for your library staff and administration.

Keeping track of your social media statistics can assist you in proving the value of this essentially free advertising to your administration, and can justify the inclusion for social media manager responsibilities as part of a staff member's job description or as justification for a full or part-time marketing position in your library.

Responding to Social Media Users

What are people saying about your hashtag and your discovery system online? The benefit of social media is that it allows everyone to have a voice, but the anonymity of the online world can sometimes make people feel free to make negative comments without worrying about the consequences. You will receive responses to your social media posts that can range from glowing accolades to positive comments, to cranky complaints, to ugly messages, sometimes all in the same day! Not surprisingly, most of your responses will come from people who have strong opinions. You will not hear from the great majority who don't have a strong opinion one way or another. You'll need to monitor your social media traffic so that you can maintain a two-way flow of information with your patrons, and so that you'll be aware if a negative trend has bubbled up in response to your posts. You can't control what people put on social media or how they respond, but the good thing about working in the library field is that it's a much less controversial environment than other polarizing fields like government or newspapers. Chances are slim that your posts will garner negative attention, but you'll need to be aware if unexpected responses are posted.

Responding to the glowing and good is easy; you just have to remember to answer each and every message. Online responders are a lot like siblings, it will be noticed if you respond to one and not the others. Luckily, it doesn't take much to acknowledge a positive contact. A quick "We are looking forward to it too!" or "Thanks!" or even a smiley emoticon will suffice. If you receive a lot of love immediately after a posting, you can post a generic "Thanks for all the positive thoughts about our new discovery system!" rather than responding to each post individually. If you haven't considered using a social media dashboard, note that they allow you to respond to posts, tweets, and pins without opening each social media interface. This can be a tremendous lifesaver when responding to user comments and inquiries.

Responding to bad and ugly comments can be more challenging than answering positive comments and question. There are many reasons that a person might choose to post a negative comment:

- The user may be responding because they had a bad experience with your library or your discovery system.
- They may have had bad experiences with other libraries' systems in the past.
- They may see your implementation of a discovery system as a waste of money (tuition or taxpayer).
- Or they may just be generally unhappy and want to vent about it.

Responding to these comments requires some tact and several deep breaths. It helps to start by acknowledging that you received their message and stating that the library is always looking for ways to improve systems and services. It is important for other online users to see that you have responded to the negative comment so that they will know that your library is open to constructive criticism. You can de-escalate the situation by not refuting the negative post and by not engaging in a confrontation. A good way to diffuse the situation is to write something like "I would like to hear more of your suggestions for library improvements. Please contact me offline at _insert e-mail address_____." The odds are that you won't hear from them again, but at least you showed that you were open to discussing the problem. If the post is especially nasty, note that most social media outlets offer a way to delete or hide posts from other users, but be cautious in choosing to do so. You obviously do not want posts filled with offensive ideas and language sitting on your feed, but you also don't want to be accused of hiding negative comments and not responding to legitimate patron concerns.

When reviewing patron posts on your social media feeds, pay attention to what they are saying. If everything is good, be sure to let the entire library staff know, because their efforts have contributed to the library's positive reception in the community. If the comments are bad, make sure to follow up and investigate the claims. See whether any of the negative posts are a trend, and try to find ways that the circumstances that led to the complaints can be fixed. If you are able to fix a problem, broadcast it on social media so that your followers can see that their comments are valued and taken seriously. Optimizing your discovery system means engaging in continual monitoring of patron feedback and improvement based on this feedback.

Rollout Events

A rollout event, whether large or small, can be a fun way to draw attention to your new or improved discovery system. It can be a small affair with cake and a few balloons, or it can be part of a larger event like an annual library open house. One of the biggest decisions to make is when to hold the rollout. Does the rollout have to take place on the actual implementation date? No, it doesn't, and quite frankly, there are a great number of reasons why it shouldn't. Implementation dates are seldom written in concrete. A million things could come up that change the date, and if you had scheduled the rollout to coincide with your implementation date, you'd need to cancel cakes, balloons, and try to contact every person who heard about the original date and time. Also, if you chose the official implementation day as the day for the rollout party, keep in mind that a great number of staff will be unavailable for the party because they'll be busy monitoring and troubleshooting the new system.

Here are a few rollout tips:

Advertising: Put your brand hashtag to use. Either create a new hashtag by placing the word "event" at the end of the original, or simply flood social media with news of the event and use the original one. Set up an event on Facebook and ask library staff to accept the event invitation and share it with their friends lists. Also, make sure that event information is included on the hashtag informational web page. Social media advertising can even continue during the day and time of the event. We live in a very spur-of-the-moment world. Ask library staff members to tweet that they are attending the event as it is going on and you may be surprised at the number of last-minute attendees who are drawn in.

Promotional items: You will get the most promotional mileage out of items that can be used on a daily or weekly basis, so that your discovery system name or hashtag is in front of the user frequently. Small credit card sleeves, sometimes referred to as ID wallets, are an inexpensive giveaway and very useful for holding a college

ID or library card. Keychains or lanyards are also the type of item carried daily. Study and research-related items also have library appeal. Small containers of sticky notes, highlighters, and clip-on book lights can all be imprinted with your logo. If you have items left over after your rollout event, you can continue to make them available to your patrons at your service desks, or in high traffic areas like printer and computer locations. Even something small like having pencils printed with the logo and placed next to piles of scrap paper at the public terminals is a positive PR move.

Add an educational element: Cake and promotional items are a big draw, but once you lure patrons to your event, you'll want to provide them with a chance to try out the system that you're promoting. Make sure that you have ample opportunity for demonstrations and actual patron use. This may mean setting up extra laptops and tablets for the event, and you will want to recruit staff to help patrons try out the discovery system and troubleshoot any technology problems that might pop up.

Staff kudos: Don't forget to celebrate the library staff at the event. As much as we want our patrons to embrace the system, it is the staff that has sacrificed the most for its implementation and will be most impacted by its existence. Be sure to thank everyone who participated in the planning, testing, and promotion of the system. Consider giving staff paper plate awards, or special badges, or any other fun recognition that you can devise.

DISCOVERY SYSTEM ORIENTATION

If your discovery system has been in place for a while, but you're not getting the usage that you'd like to see, consider hosting some system orientations. If you work in a school or college library, each new school year will bring a fresh crop of students and teachers who may be unfamiliar with your discovery system. You may also have new employees who started after the discovery system implementation, or new community patrons or volunteers. If you prefer to not schedule stand-alone sessions, consider partnering with the planners of events like new employee orientation, freshman orientation, or other scheduled events. Each of these is an opportunity to introduce, demonstrate, and emphasize the importance of your discovery system. Make sure that the system name has been significantly promoted during the session and, if possible, give each participant a promotional takeaway like a bookmark or magnet. Make sure to cover the location of the library's social media outlets and web pages so that people will know where to go to keep current with library updates and events. You can even designate time during the session for participants to pull out their phones and add the sites on the spot.

Promotional Timing

One thing to remember about promoting your discovery system is that library clientele constantly changes, so the patrons who heard about the new system when it launched may not be the same patrons who come to the library in three months. This is especially true in a school or college environment where a new batch of freshmen or middle school/high school students comes in every year. The branding, defining, and instruction of the discovery system cannot be a one-shot, three-month rollout that then disappears. Each incoming class will need the same introduction to your system every year.

COMMUNITY BUY-IN
Library Staff

Ironically, selling the discovery system to librarians and library staff can be much harder than gaining library patron buy-in. The concept of the discovery system and its "one-stop shopping" promise can lead to anxiety and fear for your colleagues and staff because it means that their daily workflow could be affected and the changes could impact their positions. Not all these fears are unfounded. Anyone who's worked in the library field for more than a couple of years has been through large projects that required huge amounts of time and effort but then eventually failed and faded away. If you've experienced this kind of frustration, it can be hard to muster excitement and enthusiasm the next time a big project comes around. Another big fear that can be sparked by the implementation of a discovery system is the familiar "librarians will become obsolete" concern. This fear is constantly stoked by news stories in the media about how the public can find anything online and libraries are no longer needed. When trying to engage buy-in from your staff, be respectful of their concerns, but try to remind them that the flip side of new technology developments is that they offer new opportunities to help our patrons find what they need.

New library systems sometimes bring a fear of change for library staff, and even for some patrons, and can lead to a strong desire to stick with the tried and true old way of doing things. The idea of a new system can be unwelcome to seasoned veterans who have lived through one or more iterations of their OPAC and various mutations of their integrated library system. These individuals do not want to hear soothing words and slick presentations from discovery system salespeople. To truly get buy-in from this group, you will need to bring in library staff from local libraries who have already lived through the process and who can speak frankly about the good, bad, and the ugly aspects of the change. You'll want to recruit outside staff who have an overall positive take on the outcome, but they don't need to shy away from the realities of the implementation. Forewarned is forearmed, and if your colleagues are given specific information about how the new system will affect them, they may be more willing to support its use. Consortia listservs, conference sessions, journal articles, and other sources of information from current users of your discovery system can also provide a wealth of honest reviews. Encourage your staff to use their research skills to find published and informal feedback on your discovery system product.

All your colleagues and staff want to feel needed, and want reassurance that the new system will not replace their jobs. Reference and instruction librarians may be most concerned about the new system because it will impact their daily life more than other library staff. They may have legitimate concerns about the quality of the data in the discovery system and the way in which it's presented. While they're probably aware of the fact that most patrons use Google or other single-search platforms to find answers to general questions, they may disagree with taking a single-search approach in the library. Many librarians believe that we should provide a higher standard of research for our patrons than an Internet search engine. Try to work with these staff members and explain that the implementation of the discovery system doesn't mean that it will be the only place to do research. They can still teach and promote specialized databases in their instruction sessions and at library service points. Show your colleagues the benefits of the discovery system, and demonstrate how it's a good starting point for general research questions and for new patrons who are unfamiliar with the somewhat clunky interfaces of traditional library catalogs and databases. Make sure to listen to the concerns of your librarians and staff, and don't discount them, even if you know that their disapproval will not stop the system from being implemented. If your staff are not on board with the new system, it will impact whether or not they promote it to your patrons, and that can severely affect usage for your system.

The discovery system, as with any newly introduced feature, will require an orientation for users and a certain amount of instruction and ongoing assistance. Highlight this point to your colleagues and staff, and show how rather than replacing their traditional work, it will actually give them more to do in the classroom and at service points because all your patrons will be unfamiliar with the new system. You can also encourage your staff and colleagues to take a positive look at the discovery system by pointing out the advantages of the single-search bar, and by showing them how it has the potential to eliminate many of the most basic questions, which will give them more time to work with patrons on more difficult research projects. The discovery system is a dramatic step toward easier research for your patrons, and librarians and library staff can show their willingness to keep up with the changing world by helping patrons to use the new system.

Selling to Faculty

If you work in a college setting, your discovery system's acceptance among faculty will likely be divided along a generational timeline, although that is not always the case. Acceptance of new technology is often as much a personality trait as a matter of age. That being said, new, recent-graduate faculty will probably have had more experience with online research than your more senior faculty. There is a fair chance that most of your young faculty used some type of discovery system at their last academic institution. This familiarity should lead them to be more accepting of your new system than faculty who are less familiar with online research methods. It is best to make your introductory presentation about the new system in a mixed group of peers (i.e., a faculty senate meeting, department/division meeting, or faculty in-service day at a high/elementary school) so that faculty members who have used this technology in the past can share their experiences with those who may be less familiar with it. With any luck, at least one previous user will speak up to share their enthusiasm for the project. It might even be worth meeting with library-friendly faculty before your formal presentation, to let them know about the new system and to lay the groundwork for your discussion with a bigger group. It's not a terrible idea to have a few "plants" in your audience.

When describing the discovery system to faculty in a presentation, stress the ease of use for their students and the increased access to resources for the faculty member's own research. Make sure to demonstrate the scholarly limiters and filters. Just because the new system is easier to use than traditional databases, it doesn't mean that it's less rigorous academically. Demonstrate how the discovery system can be used in conjunction with more traditional, scholarly databases, and how their students can limit their results to material that originally came from other databases like JSTOR. If you run into faculty resistance to the new system and if you've been in the library field for a couple of decades, the objections that you hear may harken back to faculty fears from the days when databases replaced print indexes. We survived those changes, and we'll survive these innovations as well.

It's not always possible to meet with all your teachers or faculty members in person, so you'll need to plan to provide faculty with a preview of the discovery system and a countdown to its implementation, whether or not they'll be able to attend your in-person presentation. All your messages about the upcoming changes should emphasize the implementation date, so that users can anticipate the system's arrival and not be surprised to see the discovery system search feature magically appear one day. You can also send periodic e-mails to your faculty listservs following the implementation. It may be helpful to script a number of these publicity blurbs in advance and schedule them to be distributed weekly or monthly. Start by creating a bulleted list of discovery system highlights and benefits and send these out one at a time. In all correspondence, be sure to emphasize that their students will appreciate the discovery system's ease of use and one-stop shopping. If traditional links to the catalog and databases will continue to be available on your website, it will help to emphasize that in your message so that faculty know that they won't lose any resources with the implementation of the new system.

Here are some concerns that your faculty may have about the new system:

Change is hard: Like many of us, your faculty may exhibit an unwillingness to learn something new and may find comfort in sticking with the familiar. These tendencies are what lead faculty to teach from the same book for decades or continue to use outdated VHS tapes long into the days of streaming video (don't ask how we know that this happens).

Academic rigor: Some faculty will cling to the concept that research should be a grueling, long-suffering process. If your older faculty thought that searching one database was "too easy" as compared to reviewing individual print indexes, a single search covering hundreds of databases and the library catalog will not make them feel any better.

Subject-specific scholarship: Because the discovery system searches everything, subject area specialists may worry that the names and prestige of key databases or specific journal titles for their major or discipline may get lost in the shuffle. Leading students to discipline-specific databases and emphasizing the importance of the leading journals in their field is seen by many faculty members as an important part of their teaching mission. For this group it is important to stress the limiting features of the discovery system to assure them that this type of searching is still possible.

While the interdisciplinary nature of the discovery system may disturb some faculty, it will be refreshing to others. There has been a movement in academia to recognize the interdisciplinary aspects in all types of research. With this movement, there is a call for more assignments and more courses to be co-taught and identified as being truly interdisciplinary. For those faculties who are interested in this type of work, you can demonstrate how well the discovery system works for this kind of project by pointing out the journal names that appear on the results list for any search. For example, a search on "aliens" in a discovery system like Proquest's Summon results in articles from journals as varied as the *Canadian Association of Radiologists Journal, Stanford Law Review, Biological Invasions*, and the *History Workshop Journal*.

Citation Searching

You may find that selling faculty on promoting the discovery system to their students is easier than getting them to utilize it for their own research. In addition to the reasons previously listed, faculty may also be turned off by discovery systems because of the difficulty of performing a citation search within the system. Due to the nature of their research, faculty members are much more likely than students to know the title, author, and publication details of a specific source for their research. Normally, the more information you know, the easier it is to find an item. However, the search features in discovery systems can become overwhelmed with large amounts of data, and can result in a null search if there is even one small inconsistency (like a missing apostrophe) between the search entry and the system's knowledge base, or too much additional punctuation or formatting in the search fields. Discovery systems are great for general, entry-level searching, but they can be frustrating for power searchers who are looking for a particular article.

When you review your monthly discovery system search terms analytics, you will probably find examples of complete citations that have been cut and pasted into the search field. We live in a cut and paste world and users do not realize the sensitive natures of our search environments. While discovery system companies are aware of the problem and are working on improvements in this area, it's still problematic. In approaching this issue with your faculty, you need to identify it as a roadblock that they may encounter, and offer best practices for citation searching.

When a citation search is needed, this is the time to promote the discovery system's advanced search options. An effective demonstration is to cut and paste a complete citation from the Internet and place it in the basic search box. Allow the search to fail. Next, ask your audience to select the most unique words from the title. Try to get them to choose the most descriptive, nongeneric terms. Add those words in the title field. Next, insert the first author's last name only in the author field. A big mistake with the cut and paste method is that many academic articles have three or more authors. Depending on the citation style, they may have most or all of these authors listed. However, the discovery system may not list all of the authors and the additional name(s) listed may be what nullifies the search. This abbreviated title + author search should bring up the desired results. An additional search that is often successful is a basic search on the first author's full name plus the year range limit function to limit to the exact year of publication. Few authors are so prolific that the known citation will not appear in the first 10 results.

Be Prepared to Defend Your Data Decisions

As discussed in Chapter 3, there are a number of nontraditional sources that you can choose to include in your discovery system. These may include websites, Wikipedia entries, and reference book entries and definitions. It is possible that some of your faculty members may have railed against some of these sources in their classroom, and they may not accept papers that use websites like Wikipedia as a reference. As with controversial books in your collection, be prepared to explain and defend your discovery system data inclusion choices to your faculty members. Just because you use a Research Starter from Wikipedia to give patrons a brief overview of topic, it doesn't mean that you would encourage your patrons to use that source for a scholarly paper. The last thing you want is a faculty member to forbid their students to use your discovery system for class assignments. Students may often appear to not be paying attention in class, but that will be the one thing they will remember. How many times have you had a student tell you at the Reference Desk that they can't use a database to find articles because their faculty member told them that they can't use Internet sources? Students have a hard time telling the difference between types of online sources, and a faculty prohibition on parts of your discovery system could make students fearful to use it to find sources.

If a faculty member approaches you with a complaint, be willing to explain your position, but also consider modifying your system to better suit their educational needs. These additional sources are often displayed on the screen in unique ways to demonstrate their difference from traditional research sources like books and articles. These results may appear in a shaded area or in a right or left frame, separate from the normal results list. If that is the case, emphasize to the faculty member that students can be instructed to ignore these special sections. Students can often also hide these additional sources by clicking on a simple limit option. If the faculty member feels strongly that some of your add-ons are not "strictly academic," remind them that they can demonstrate a discovery system search in class and use it as a teachable moment to explain to students the intricacies and various levels of academic research.

Spreading the Word

One of the most effective ways to market your discovery system is by word of mouth. Try to find an influential person outside of the library who is interested in new library technology, and who would be willing to share information about your discovery system. At the college/university level this may be an instructional designer, at the k-12 level it may be a teacher known for their innovation, at the public library it may be some influential Friends of the Library who would like to spread the word about your system. It is well worth your time to identify and seek out these individuals. Offer them a personal invitation to attend discovery system workshops or invite them for a private, one-on-one session.

EMBEDDABLE CODE

If you work at a school or college library, make sure that you tell your influential people about any system widgets that can be embedded in assignments. Create print and online instructions for embedding widgets and demonstrate how to do it, if possible. If you work in a college and your course management system administrators and instructional designers are open to collaboration with the library, work with them to create policies that mandate the addition of a library discovery system widget in each online course, syllabus, or assignment.

Student Buy-In

In the school or college library environment, you will probably find that students will accept your discovery system more willingly than your teachers, faculty, and library staff. The odds are great that they have already been exposed to a discovery system in their high school or public library. They have also grown up in a Google world and know exactly what to do with a blank search box, or at least they think they do. As was discussed in previous chapters, it is important to explain to students what the discovery system is and what it isn't. It isn't a total Internet search, and it is not a site search of your library or institution's website. Overall, students will easily accept your discovery system implementation, and they will adapt quickly to any major changes that you make to the function, or look and feel, over the years.

Chapter 6

Conclusion

Discovery systems are a great way to make your licensed resources more accessible for your patrons. These resources are expensive to purchase and take staff time to manage, so you want to be sure that they're being found and used by the library patrons who need them.

YOU HAVE THE POWER

When we're handed a new out-of-the-box library tool, it's easy to accept it as is. Most of us are busy and don't have the time to think about ways that the tool could work better for us—we're just trying to get it working and then train our patrons how to use it. We hope that this book has given you some ideas for ways to start taking more control of your systems and how they work. Usability testing is the first step in figuring out what's working well with your discovery system, what's a problem for some people but not for others, and where you really need to make some changes. Without gathering usability data, it's difficult to identify specific problems, and without that information, it's hard to know how to begin to change things and improve service for your patrons.

Usability data for your discovery system can help you at all levels. Are you a one-person shop where you are able to control your own discovery system administration? The data will tell you what you need to adjust and fix. Are you a librarian at a branch campus, or do you work at a large, silo-ed institution where you do not directly control your discovery system settings or web page design? You'll get a lot farther with your requests for change if you are able to back up those requests with actual data, such as "75 percent of patrons tested could not find the link to the discovery system on the library homepage." The same holds true for update requests for vendors. If you're dissatisfied with the way that your vendor's tool displays eBooks, you'll have more of a chance of getting that fixed if you have video evidence of the way that your patrons try to navigate the system. A picture and a video are worth a thousand words, and that data may be what it takes to move your request onto a vendor's enhancement schedule.

If you can define the particular ways in which your system is not meeting your needs, you'll be much more likely to succeed in fixing those problems. This holds true for working with your colleagues as well as with your discovery system administrators or vendors. Did your usability testing show that patrons are unfamiliar with your brand? You can use the statistics from your studies to show your colleagues that you're not seeing as much familiarity with the system as you'd hoped to see, and you can encourage them to be more vigilant in promoting the system at service desks and in instruction sessions.

A MOVING TARGET

Library technology changes constantly and it can be difficult to keep up with new systems, both practically and emotionally. Change is not easy, but it can be invigorating if you're open to it. The most important thing to remember is that library technology is designed to work well for the average library. The product will not come out of the box set up for your specialized location. That's where your expertise comes into play. No one knows your patron base better than you and your colleagues at the library. You are the people who interact with your patrons every day, and you are going to be the best judges of how to make the system work best for your particular location. You can implement the usability tools covered in this book to gather data to back up your practical knowledge about your patrons, and you can use your native intelligence and usability data to design, teach, and promote the best possible discovery system configuration for **your** patrons at **your** library. The only constant is change, but if you can remain connected to and aware of your patrons' research needs, you can continue to provide excellent service and support to them, regardless of the exact nature of the research technology.

Appendix: Software and Tools

DISCOVERY SYSTEM PRODUCTS (HIGHEST SALES)

EBSCO Discovery System (EDS): Discovery system product created, hosted, and maintained by EBSCO: https://www.ebscohost.com/discovery

Primo: Search and delivery tool from Ex Libris, who was recently purchased by Proquest: http://www.exlibrisgroup.com/category/PrimoOverview

Summon: Web-scale discovery system tool from Proquest: http://www.proquest.com/products-services/The-Summon-Service.html

Worldcat Discovery: OCLC's discovery system, works with their Worldshare platform: https://www.oclc.org/worldcat-discovery.en.html

USABILITY SOFTWARE

Camtasia: Screen capture and tutorial building software from Techsmith, already in use at many libraries: https://www.techsmith.com/camtasia.html

FocusGroupIT: Free online focus group software, can help force equal participation across group: https://www.focusgroupit.com/

Google Analytics: Popular web analytics software that can be used to track library web pages usage: https://www.google.com/analytics

itracks: Tool for online focus groups, communities, IDIs, and surveys: https://www.itracks.com/

Jing: Free screen capture tool from Techsmith, good for short sessions: http://www.techsmith.com/jing.html

Morae: User experience and market research software from Techsmith: https://www.techsmith.com/morae.html

Optimizely: A/B testing and personalization platform for the web and mobile apps: https://www.optimizely.com/

Poll Everywhere: Audience response system that uses Twitter, mobile phones, and the web: https://www.polleverywhere.com

StudioCode: Video recording software from Digital Tec Solutions designed to help you code videos to track behavior or actions: http://www.dtsvideo.com/studiocode

SurveyMonkey: Free online survey tool: https://www.surveymonkey.com/

EDUCATION SOFTWARE

Blackboard: Commonly used academic course management software: http://www
.blackboard.com

Moodle: Open source course management system and learning platform: https://
moodle.org/

LIBRARY SOFTWARE

LibGuides: Springshare's web content management tool for libraries; options include
chat, statistical package, calendar tool, and form/survey creation: https://www
.springshare.com/libguides/

PR SOFTWARE AND VENDORS

Canva: Photo editing and professional, graphic design creation: https://www.canva.com/

Fotor: Photo editing and collage creation: http://www.fotor.com/

OpenClipart: Public domain clipart collection for commercial and noncommercial
use: https://openclipart.org/

Pixabay: Public domain collection of high-quality photos and film: https://pixabay
.com/

Google Image Search: Comprehensive search across the Internet, not all images in
the public domain, also offers a "reverse image search": https://images.google
.com/

Hashtagify: Large hashtag search engine, also shows tracking and usage patterns:
http://hashtagify.me/

Hootsuite: Social media management tool that allows you to monitor a variety of
outlets at once and monitor your outreach: https://hootsuite.com/

Sendible: Management tool offers monitoring and interacting with users through a
social media dashboard: http://sendible.com/

Tagboard: Displays tagged posts from Facebook, Twitter, and Instagram: https://
tagboard.com/

PRESENTATION TOOLS

Piktochart: Free infographics tool for reports, presentations, and other visual presentations: https://piktochart.com/

Snipping Tool/Apple Screen Capture: Used to copy user-defined areas of your computer screen, comes with Windows and Apple PCs and laptops

Glossary

A/B Testing—A method used to compare the results of two versions of the same web page or application. Over a specific amount of time, an audience of web users is randomly given one of two versions of the same web resource and studies are made to conclude which was more effective from a user standpoint.

Analytics—A means to collect and analyze reportable data from your website or web application. Analytics answer the who, what, where, and when questions about entry and use of your website.

Beta Testing—The last round of testing, usually with potential users or a small focus group, before a product is released to the full audience.

Card Sorting—A low-tech approach to obtaining user feedback on web design. Researchers write concepts or terms on individual pieces of paper (index cards, sticky notes) and ask individuals to place them in similar groupings or place them under predefined categories.

Consent Form—A document, usually requiring a research participant's signature, stating their willingness to participate in a study. Consent forms often contain details about the study, any potential risks, and information concerning the potential use of individual study results (i.e., publication or as part of a larger study).

Direct Observation—A researcher's physical observation of a study participant doing an action or completing a task in the participant's own environment, without interacting with the participant.

Eye Tracking—The process of monitoring eye movements to see on which elements of a website or web application that a user is scanning or concentrating.

Focus Group—A small group of people brought together for a moderated meeting to discuss opinions or reflections on a product or activity.

Heat Mapping—Creation of a graphical representation of data that shows amounts of activity on screen as colors.

Heuristic Evaluation—Having a small group of individuals familiar with usability testing review a website to make sure it is in compliance with basic, accepted usability principles.

Indirect Observation—Research conducted not by the researcher directly observing the participant. Collecting observations from others, videotaped recordings, and screen capture video taken when the researcher was not present are examples of indirect observation.

Infographics Visual representations that represent numerical research findings and other data such as charts and graphs.

Institutional Review Board—A committee formed to review and approve proposed research projects. In particular, these committees are charged with seeing that ethical and humane methods are in place and followed for the protection of research participants.

Personas—Written profiles created to represent particular subgroups of web users for usability purposes. Personas should be a composite based on characteristics of individuals in that subgroup.

Qualitative Method—Use of nonnumerical, observational data to arrive at research conclusions.

Quantitative Method—Use of measurable statistical and numerical data to arrive at research conclusions.

Screen Capture Recording—The internal taping of user interaction with a computer.

Search Engine Optimization—The process of making a website or web page more visible by manipulating search engines so that the site is listed higher on a search engine results list.

Social Media—Online-based sites dedicated to communicating and sharing ideas through community-based computer interaction.

Usability Lab Study—Research on user interaction conducted in a controlled setting such as a computer lab, usually with multiple participants at one time.

Widget—A small application that can be added onto a website and allows the user to directly interact with a much larger application elsewhere on the web.

Bibliography

Breeding, Marshall. "Disintegration to Integration and Back." *Computers in Libraries* 36.2 (2016): 25–29.

Breeding, Marshall. "Library Technology Guides." http://librarytechnology.org/discovery/. Accessed August 22, 2016.

Collier, Ellie. "EBSCO Discovery Service Integrations, Custom Solutions, & Upcoming Enhancements." PowerPoint presentation at SUNYLA Annual Meeting, Binghamton, NY, June 9, 2016.

Coca Cola Commercial. "I'd Like to Teach the World to Sing (In Perfect Harmony)." YouTube. 1971. https://www.youtube.com/watch?v=ib-Qiyklq-Q.

Derla, Katherine. "More Than 90 Percent of College Students Prefer Reading Paper Books over e-Books." *Tech Times*. 2016. http://www.techtimes.com/articles/131055/20160205/more-than-90-percent-of-c]ollege-students-prefer-reading-paper-books-over-e-books.htm.

EBSCO. "Do Your Students Speak Library-ese?" EBSCO Blog Post. December 11, 2015. https://www.ebsco.com/blog/article/do-your-students-speak-library-ese.

EBSCO Information Services. "User Research." https://www.ebsco.com/why-ebsco/user-research. Accessed July 18, 2016.

EBSCO. "ILS Partners." https://www.ebscohost.com/discovery/catalog/ils-partners. Accessed August 22, 2016.

Germanna Libraries. "Library Instruction at Germanna: Learning Outcomes & Library Instruction." Germanna Community College. 2016. http://germanna.libguides.com/libraryinstruction.

Imler, Bonnie, and Michelle Eichelberger. "Commercial Database Design vs. Library Terminology Comprehension: Why Do Students Print Abstracts Instead of Full-Text Articles?" *College and Research Libraries* 75.3 (2014): 284–297.

Imler, Bonnie, and Michelle Eichelberger. "Do They 'Get It'? Student Usage of SFX Citation Linking Software." *College and Research Libraries* 72.5 (2011): 454–463.

Imler, Bonnie, and Michelle Eichelberger. "Using Screen Capture to Study User Research Behavior." *Library Hi-Tech* 29.3 (2011): 446–454.

Imler, Bonnie, Neuwirth, Eddie, and Jeffrey Wisniewski. "Discovery Easy, Delivery Critical." PowerPoint presentation at Internet Librarian, Monterey, CA, October 27, 2014.

Muldoon, Pamela. "An In-Depth Look at How to Create and Use B2B Buyer Personas with Ardath Albee." Content Marketing Institute. June 4, 2012. http://contentmarketinginstitute.com/2012/06/b2b-buyer-personas-ardath-albee/.

Nielsen, Jakob. "Quantitative Studies: How Many Users to Test?" Nielsen Norman Group. 2006. https://www.nngroup.com/articles/quantitative-studies-how-many-users/.

Oxford College Library. "Student Learning Outcomes." Emory University. 2016. http://oxford.library.emory.edu/research-learning/instruction-classes/learning-outcomes.html.

Portland State University Library. "Library Instruction Program Learning Outcomes." Portland State University. http://library.pdx.edu/wp-content/uploads/library_instruction_outcomes.pdf.

Price, Jason S., and Cindi Trainor. "Digging Into the Data: Exposing the Causes of Resolver Failure." *Library Technology Reports* 46.7 (2010): 15–26.

ProQuest. "360 Link: New Technology Improves the Linking Experience." http://media2.proquest.com/documents/D4867–360-Link-Enhancements-Datasheet.pdf. Accessed September 12, 2016.

Serenity Prayer. https://en.wikipedia.org/wiki/Serenity_Prayer.

Thompson, JoLinda. *Implementing Web-Scale Discovery Services: A Practical Guide for Librarians*. Lanham, MD: Rowman & Littlefield, 2014.

Index

Abstracts, defining. *See* Terminology

A/B testing: online, 24–25; in-person, 25–26

Algorithms. *See* Search algorithms

Analytics: exit pages, 34–35; landing pages, 34–35, 69, 72–73, 103; referrer types, 34, 72; search term tracking, 32–33, 60, 72; site traffic, 32; visitor statistics, 32–33

APA citation. *See* Citations, instruction on

Apps. *See* User interface

Archival records. *See* Catalogs, local

Audio recording. *See* Data collection

Authentication. *See* User interface

Autocorrect. *See* User interface

Automated query expansion. *See* User interface

Banners, physical, use in PR. *See* Public relations

Benchmarking. *See* Web design

Best bet recommendations. *See* User interface

Beta testing. *See* Web implementation

Bibliographic instruction. *See* Instruction methods

Bibliographic standards. *See* Catalogs, local

Bibliographic tools. *See* User interface

Bing, 34

BlackBoard. *See* Course management systems

Bookmarks. *See* Public relations

Boolean operators. *See* Searching, instruction on

Branding: brainstorming, 99, 109; contest, 39, 99; enhancers, 98; local knowledge, 98; longevity, 101–2; name promotion, 97–106; name recognition, 101–2; name selection, 99–100; polls, 15, 18–20; superlatives, 98

Brodart. *See* Catalogs, local

Breeding, Marshall, 1–2

Bucket testing. *See* A/B testing

Camtasia. *See* Techsmith

Canva, 104

Card sorting, 20–21, 41, 58

Catalogs, external: consortia, 51

Catalogs, local: live searching, 49; OCLC holdings, 50–51; tools, 51–52; updates, 49–50

Chat, 2, 31, 62–63, 72, 91–92

CINAHL, 53, 59, 86

Citations, instruction on, 90

Citation tools. *See* User interface

Cloud data, 2, 46, 60

Coding, data: design, 41–42; short-cut keys, 42; timelines, adding, 42

Cognitive walkthough. *See* Study instruments

Confidentiality. *See* Permission, gaining for study

Configuration, discovery system: data decisions, 47–49

Consent forms: design, 7, 35; use with children, 35

Content provider, instruction on. *See* Limiting, instruction on

Contextual help. *See* User interface

Convenience sampling. *See* Sample method

Countdowns. *See* Public relations

Course management systems: BlackBoard, 2, 34, 67; Moodle, 2, 34, 67

Crazy Egg. *See* Heat mapping

Credo (database), 54, 61, 89

Currency, ranking. *See* Result ranking, instruction on; User interface

Data analysis: advanced, 41; manual, 41; software, 41. *See also* Coding, data

Database recommendations, instruction on, 87–88

Databases: keyword triggers, 52–53; recommended database option in Summon, 52–53, 87–88; selection, 53–54; specialized content, 52

Data collection: audio recording, 28–29; eye tracking, 28; logistics, 28–29; video recording, 28–29. *See also* Direct observation; Indirect observation; Screen capture

Data retention: destroying data, 46; format, 45; future studies, 45; IRB requirements, 45; privacy, 39, 45; storage methods, 45–46

Dialog (database), 74

Digital collections. *See* Catalogs, local

Direct observation: note taking, 26–27; research paths, 26; tracking behavior, 26–27. *See also* Consent forms

EasyBib, 90

eBook collections: access, 54–55, 86; filters, 54–55; selection, 54

EBSCO: curriculum building, 2; EDS, 1–3, 33, 49–50, 52, 54, 56–63, 79, 81, 83, 84–89, 91–92, 94, 99; user research group, 5, 58

EDS. *See* EBSCO

Electronic signage, use in PR. *See* Public relations

E-mail, use in PR. *See* Public relations

EndNote, 90

Exit pages. *See* Analytics

Ex Libris: Primo, 1

External referrer. *See* Analytics

Eye tracking. *See* Data collection

Facebook, 60, 104, 106–8, 111, 114

Facets and filters: selection, 58–62; terminology, 58; working with vendor, 59–62

Faculty, generating buy-in: building alliances, 121; citation searching, 119–20; data decisions, 120–21; group presentations, 118; one-on-one demonstrations, 118; selling points, 118

Federated searching, 1

Filters. *See* Facets and filters

Findings, reporting: demonstrations, 43–44; infographics, 43; recommendations, 43–44

FocusGroupIt. *See* Focus groups

Focus groups: beta site testing, 68; instead of personas, 13; moderating, 21–22; observation, 22–23; participants, 21; preparation, 21; questions, 22–24; software, 22

Formal sampling. *See* Sample method

Format, instruction on. *See* Limiting, instruction on

Fotor, 104

Free-range searching. *See* Usability lab

Gale Virtual Reference Library (database), 54, 61

General education learning outcomes. *See* Learning outcomes

Geographic limiting, instruction on. *See* Limiting, instruction on

Goodreads. *See* Google

Google: Goodreads, 3, 60; Google Analytics, 25, 33; Google Books, 3, 60

Grit. *See* Research grit

Handouts, instruction, 101

Hashtagify, 112

Hashtags: design, 108–9; monitoring, 111–12; peer review, 109; use in PR, 109–11, 114–15

Heat mapping: 80/20 rule, 31; duration/ timing, 30; software, 30; use for web design, 30–32

Help, discovery system, 72, 90–91

Heuristic evaluation. *See* Study instruments

Hootsuite, 111–12

HTML full-text, defining. *See* Terminology

Human participants. *See* Study participants

IEDL. *See* Link resolvers

Index-enhanced direct linking. *See* Link resolvers

Indirect observation, 30. *See also* Analytics; Heat mapping

Infographics. *See* Findings, reporting

Information literacy. *See* Instruction methods

Instagram, 104, 108

Institutional review board (IRB), 7–8, 35–37, 45

Institutional student learning outcomes. *See* Learning outcomes

Instruction methods, 74

Instruments. *See* Study instruments

Interlibrary loan, 2, 24, 33, 50, 62–63, 86

Internal referrers. *See* Analytics

Itracks. *See* Focus groups

Jargon. *See* Terminology

Jing. *See* Techsmith

JSTOR (database), 33, 53–54, 57, 59–60, 86, 118

Keyword searching, instruction. *See* Searching, instruction on

Landing page. *See* Analytics

Language limiting, instruction on. *See* Limiting, instruction on

Learning outcomes: assessment, 74–75; examples, 75

LibGuides. *See* Springshare

Librarian recommendations, instruction on, 88

Library-ese. *See* Terminology

LibraryH3lp, 91

Library holdings, instruction on. *See* Limiting, instruction on

Library staff, generating buy-in: fear of change, 116; feedback, 116; orientation, 117; outside review, 116; peer support, 117

Licensed content. *See* Authentication; Databases; eBook collections; User interface

Limiting, instruction on: by content provider, 86; by format type, 82–84; by language, 85–86; by library availability, 86–87; by publisher, 85; scholarly content, 84

Link resolvers: OpenURL, 63; placement, 62–63; terminology, 62–63

Live testing. *See* A/B testing

McNaughton collection. *See* Catalogs, local

Magnets, use in PR. *See* Public relations

MARC records. *See* Catalogs, local

Medline (database), 53, 86

Metadata, 41, 63, 72

MetaLib, 1

Methods. *See* Study method

Microsoft Excel. *See* Data analysis

Microsoft PowerPoint. *See* Findings, reporting

Microsoft Word. *See* Findings, reporting

Minitab. *See* Data analysis

MLA citation. *See* Citations, instruction on

Moodle. *See* Course management systems

Morae. *See* Techsmith

Multivariate testing. *See* A/B testing

OCLC: Worldcat, 1, 50–51; Worldcat Local, 1, 99; Worldshare Management System, 52. *See also* Catalogs, external

Online public access catalog. *See* Catalogs, local

OPAC. *See* Catalogs, local

OpenClipart, 104

OpenURL. *See* Link resolvers

Orientations, use as PR. *See* Public relations

Participants. *See* Study participants

PDF, defining. *See* Terminology

Peer-reviewed. *See* Terminology

Peer-reviewed content, instruction on. *See* Limiting, instruction on

Permission, gaining for study: official review, 35; question of deception, 36. *See also* Institutional review board

Personas: examples, 11; representation, 13; template, 12–13

Piktochart, 43

Pixabay, 104

Placards. *See* User interface

Poll Everywhere, 19

Polls and surveys: audience, 19; branding, 19; duration, 19; question design, 19; sampling, 19; use as PR, 20

Posters, use in PR. *See* Public relations

Primo. *See* Ex Libris

Program student learning outcomes. *See* Learning outcomes

Promotion. *See* Public relations

Promotional items. *See* Public relations

Proquest: online wiki, 5; SIPX Reading List, 2; Summon, 1–3, 5, 20, 49, 52–55, 60–61, 63, 81, 83–84, 86–91, 94, 98–99, 119

Public relations: banners, physical, 110; bookmarks, 103; countdowns, 105–6; electronic signage, 105, 110; e-mails and texts, 104–5; leadership, 102–3; magnets, 109–10; online promotion, 106–14; orientations, 115; posters, 103–4; promotional items, 103, 111, 114; QR codes, 103; timing, 105, 115–16; word of mouth, 68, 121. *See also* Branding; Rollout events; Scavenger hunts; Widgets

Publisher, limiting by. *See* Limiting, instruction on

Purpose, study. *See* Study purpose

QR codes, use in PR. *See* Public relations

Qualitative method. *See* Study method

Quantitative method. *See* Study method

Quotation marks, instruction. *See* Searching, instruction on

Random sampling. *See* Sample method

Recruiting participants: anonymity, 39; funding, 38–39; incentives, 37–39; online, 36–37; in person, 36–37; volunteer sampling, 36–37

Reference desk, instruction on: online, 91–92; in person, 91–92; promotion, 91–92. *See also* Chat

Reference sources, instruction on, 88–89

Relevancy ranking. *See* Result ranking, instruction on; User interface

Research grit, teaching, 92–95

Research guides, instruction on, 88

Research starter. *See* User interface

Research starter, instruction on, 89

Result ranking, instruction on: by date, 81–82; relevancy, 80–82

Results lists: column display, 56–57; item records, 57; number of results, 57; placement, 56

Retention. *See* Data retention

Rollout events: advertising, 110, 114; giveaways, 114–15; hands-on training, 115; staff acknowledgement, 115; timing, 114

Salem Press, 54, 60

Sample method: convenience sampling, 14–15; formal sampling, 14; privacy, 14; random sampling, 14; size, 14

SAS. *See* Data analysis

Scavenger hunts, 23–24, 47–48, 107

Scholarly journal, instruction on. *See* Limiting, instruction on

Scholarly journals. *See* Terminology

Scope of study. *See* Study scope

Screen capture: mouse tracking, 27–28; screen size, 27; software, 27–28

Screenshots. *See* Findings, reporting

Search algorithms, 49, 80

Search box. *See* Web design

Search Engine Optimization (SEO): analytics, 71–72

Searching, instruction on: advanced, 77–78; Boolean, 78–79; keyword, 76–77; natural language searching, 76; quotation marks, 79; search suggestions,

79; subject, 76–77; synonyms, 77; truncation, 79–80

Search parameters, instruction on, 80–82

Search referrer. *See* Analytics

Search suggestions, instruction on. *See* Searching, instruction on

Sendible, 112

Serials solutions: 360 Search, 1

Size of sample. *See* Sample method

Smartlinks. *See* Link resolvers

Snipping Tool. *See* Findings, reporting

Social media. *See* Social networking

Social media tools. *See* User interface

Social networking: dashboards, 111–13; incentives, 107; invitations, 106–7; responding to users, 112–14; scavenger hunt, 107–8; teasers, 106, 108. *See also* Facebook; Hashtags; Twitter

Special collections. *See* Catalogs, local; Result ranking, instruction on

Sorting results. *See* User interface

Spotlighting. *See* User interface

Springshare: LibAnswers, 91; LibGuides, 2–3, 18, 34, 56, 61, 67, 88

SPSS Statistics. *See* Data analysis

StackMaps, 62

Students, generating buy-in, 121–22

StudioCode. *See* Data analysis

Study findings. *See* Findings, reporting

Study instruments: cognitive walkthough, 16–18; heuristic evaluation, 16–18. *See also* Card sorting; Focus groups; Polls and surveys; Usability lab

Study method: hybrid, 16; qualitative, 15–16, 23, 32; quantitative, 15–16, 32. *See also* Sample method

Study participants: demographics, 10–11; identifying, 10–11; sample size, 13–14. *See also* Consent forms; Personas; Recruiting participants; Sample method

Study purpose: definition, 9; negative examples, 9; positive examples, 9

Study scope: large-scale, 10; small-scale, 10

Study team: input, 8; representation, 8; size, 8

Subject searching, instruction. *See* Searching, instruction on

Suggested librarian links, 61, 88

Summon. *See* Proquest

SurveyMonkey, 19

Surveys and polls. *See* Polls and survey

Tagboard, 112

Techsmith: Camtasia, 27; Jing, 27; Morae, 19, 27–28, 42

Terminology: in filters, 58–59; instruction on, 93–94

Texts, use in PR. *See* Public relations

Thompson, JoLinda, 2

360 Link. *See* Link resolvers

360 Search. *See* Serials Solutions

360 Sidebar. *See* Link resolvers

Topic explorer. *See* User interface

Topic explorer, instruction on, 89

Truncation, instruction on. *See* Searching, instruction on

Tweets. *See* Twitter

Twitter: analytics, 112; embedding feeds, 111; retweets, 111–12; timelines, 111; tracking, 112

Usability lab: free-range searching, 24; instrument design, 24; scavenger hunt, 23–24

Usability testing: framework, 6–8; overview, 5–8

User experience (UX). *See* Usability testing

User interface: apps, 62; autocorrect, 62; automated query expansion, 60; best bet recommendations, 60–61; bibliographic tools, 60; citation tools, 60; contextual help, 62; placards, 60; relevancy ranking and sorting, 57–58; research starter, 60; social media tools, 60; spotlighting, 61; topic explorer, 61. *See also* Facets and filters; Results lists; Web design

Video recording. *See* Data collection

Web 2.0, 2

WebAim.org, 67

Web design: benchmarking, 65; search box design, 65–67; search box placement, 66–67. *See also* Widgets

Web implementation: beta testing, 67–69; rollout, 69; transition planning, 69

Widgets: design, 56; use as PR, 111; use in content management systems, 67, 121

Wikipedia, 61, 84, 89

Word of mouth, use in PR. *See* Public relations

Worldcat. *See* OCLC

Worldcat Local. *See* OCLC

Worldshare management system. *See* OCLC

Z39.50. *See* Catalogs, local

About the Authors

BONNIE IMLER is library director at Penn State Altoona, Altoona, Pennsylvania, and the web usability and assessment coordinator for Penn State University Libraries. She has been conducting studies on actual use of library resources by patrons long before the term "usability" and the acronym UX came into vogue. Imler has conducted studies on student use of full-text articles, databases, link resolvers, and eBooks. She has published articles on her usability study results and the use of screen capture video as a means to capture and analyze human-computer interaction.

MICHELLE EICHELBERGER is the systems and electronic services librarian at Genesee Community College in Batavia, New York, which is part of the State University of New York (SUNY) system. She served on the SUNY Office of Library and Information Services Task Force that reviewed options and presented recommendations for implementation of a SUNY-wide Discovery System in 2013. Eichelberger has collaborated on user research and publications with Bonnie Imler for more than a decade.

Made in United States
Orlando, FL
22 March 2026